Reflections and Recipes
Revealed

Reflections and Recipes
Revealed

Experience the Taste of Sweet Success

D.S.R

iUniverse LLC
Bloomington

REFLECTIONS AND RECIPES REVEALED
Experience the Taste of Sweet Success

iUniverse books may be ordered through booksellers or by contacting:

iUniverse LLC
1663 Liberty Drive
Bloomington, IN 47403
www.iuniverse.com
1-800-Authors (1-800-288-4677)

Because of the dynamic nature of the Internet, any web addresses or links contained in this book may have changed since publication and may no longer be valid. The views expressed in this work are solely those of the author and do not necessarily reflect the views of the publisher, and the publisher hereby disclaims any responsibility for them.

Any people depicted in stock imagery provided by Thinkstock are models, and such images are being used for illustrative purposes only. Certain stock imagery © Thinkstock.

ISBN: 978-1-4917-1940-4 (sc)
ISBN: 978-1-4917-1941-1 (e)

Printed in the United States of America.

iUniverse rev. date: 01/30/2014

Contents

Foreword

"AllerAnfang is schwer" is a German expression that means all beginnings are difficult. This certainly holds true for people who immigrate to the United States and have to understand both the language and the culture. Education is often the key to this understanding, and people who seek it will make their beginning at their new home less difficult.

When I first came to the United States from Europe, I thought I had a good grasp of the language. I had started taking English classes in 5th grade, and I was now 22. However, the experience was quite a culture shock. My first job in the United States was at Central Texas College, and when I started taking courses there, I learned quickly that my dictionary was my best friend. I always carried it in my purse. Even then, pronunciation presented problems. Once, when I found myself standing at the cash register with a "rope," and my friend had a "robe," I learned the big differences that one subtle sound can make.

I also had interesting experiences with American foods. The first time I went to a restaurant in Killeen with my friends, I was very surprised when the waiter brought me pieces of meat coated with some kind of weird crust. Where was the chicken I ordered? In Germany we usually eat rotisserie chicken, but this "fried chicken" looked and tasted nothing like it. Later, when we finished our meal, my friend paid and we immediately left the restaurant. I was wondering why we were in such a hurry and thought perhaps we were going somewhere else as a surprise for me, but to my disappointment we just went home. In German restaurants, dinners are very big and drawn out, with long conversations that usually last hours. Needless to say my learning curve about American language and culture was great.

Many immigrants experience similar language barriers and cultural differences when they arrive in the New World. My advice is to start taking English-as-A Second Language courses as soon as you arrive, like the students did who are sharing their recipes with you in this book. English-as-A Second Language courses cover basic grammar, reading and writing, and cultural studies, but moreover they give students the confidence to explore the world around them and embrace change. Every time I attend an end-of-school year celebration, English-as-A Second Language students show pride in their accomplishments and gratitude about having learned so much in the program.

I believe the important part is to explore and appreciate your new country and yet hold on to some of the traditions of your home countries. All these experiences enrich us as individuals, and they also make American culture what it is. An excellent way to express your native culture is by sharing traditional dishes with people from different cultures. This book will provide you with a wide array of recipes and will take you on an international journey.

"Guten Appetit."

Tina Ady Ph.D,
Dean, Continental and Fort Hood Campuses

Acknowledgments

I would like to give eternal gratitude to the Creator of the Universe for blessing me with the tools necessary to pursue one of my dreams and witness the fruition. My special thanks go to the students, both former and current, who have inspired and continue to inspire me to furnish a platform to voice their emotions. I am grateful to the spouses of the students who constantly provide encouragement and support throughout the sometimes difficult, frustrating but rewarding periods. I also thank Mr. Dana Quinn for the technological support and suggestions which were always welcomed and appreciated. I have to give particular thanks to "Angel" who assisted me without hesitation and at tmes seemed so enthused about this project, which inadvertently increased my motivation.

Motivation-an essential element in accomplishing a goal. Look for the second book titled "A Compilation of Emotions" in 2014.

Welcome to the United States of America.

Chapter One

A point of contention can be made that America, the land of freedom, was founded on fairness not language skills. So if immigrants meet all other requirements, should learning English be mandatory? If people choose the United States as their home, should it not be grievously important to learn English?

ESL has provoked some debate and is now a flashpoint in immigration reform. Now, an immigration law, in its infancy, states that in order to obtain citizenship, immigrants are required to speak and write English. Some immigrants are concerned with identity. People can maintain their identities and cultural values and still get the benefits of learning English (another language). We know that some of the benefits after receiving citizenship are:

* The right to vote: You will be able to become informed and understand the rights, laws and the political system of the United States.
* Obtain a U.S. passport.
* Petition for members of your family to come to the U.S.
* Apply for federal jobs etc.: Being bi-lingual can increase the chances of obtaining a better-paying job.

Another benefit from learning the language is the opportunity to become familiar with different cultures and learn how people live. This transforms the mind into a different disposition and allows you to understand and accept people for who they are and gain a perspective of the world. Knowledge is power and culture is powerful.

According to a Census Bureau report, there are 37.9 million immigrants speaking 311 languages. Many languages are used in the U. S. with English as the most commonly used. The Free Encyclopedia states that English is the Defacto national language of the U.S. with 80% of the population claiming it as a mother tongue and 45% claiming it to speak it "well" or "very well" However, no official language exists at the federal level.

Hundreds of years ago, America was founded by immigrants. Some say, without immigrants there would be no United States. Others ask: Where would immigrants be without the United States?

When immigrants flocked to the United States hundreds of years ago (still to a large extent today) a working knowledge of English was not necessary for survival. Immigrant communities were formed because of the desire to keep their cultural traditions and still be able to be involved in American life at some level. Americans tried to accommodate, but not being able to communicate with each other on the job, in schools and even in the community was frustrating and perplexing to some.

In the search for some sort of unified national identity, American congressmen and educators formed schools for English Language instruction. Congress passed the Naturalization Act in 1906, which required that immigrants be able to speak English to become naturalized as stated in The History of ESOL website.

More opportunities began to emerge to tighten the communication gap. As far back as 1914, the Ford Motor Company established The Ford English School, according to the University of Michigan Auto Life website. The school taught the company's immigrant workers how to speak English, added lessons on American history and culture and included American values.

During World War II, the United States again recognized the importance of foreign languages and foreign language education. Individuals and educators started to welcome other languages, and developed an appreciation of foreign languages and displayed encouragement to learn English into ESL education.

According to an Adult ESL specialist at the Center for Applied Linguistics (CAL) adult basic education has been federally funded since the Adult Education Act of 1966 and the 1970 amendments to that legislation that expanded educational services to include ESL and citizenship.

ESL programs exist nationwide and internationally. Some incur a fee and some do not. Sometimes, in the U.S., depending on the state, the Adult Education budgets are cut across local districts where Beginning, Intermediate and Advanced level ESL classes are normally conducted. It is quite evident, that in order for immigrants, or anyone for that matter, to learn a language, resources must be available. Here, at the Adult Education Program, qualified instructors/teachers ("teachinstors") coupled with experienced, competent administrative personnel ensure students are adequately schooled, provided with the necessary resources and the state's goals are attained.

Chapter Two

The language barrier can destroy and sometimes prohibit relationships. Some immigrants are reluctant to integrate. Assumptions should not automatically be made that some are stupid because they do not speak another person's language.

Students tell stories about the discouragement and frustration that seep in, which can become factors that impede the accomplishment of their goals. There can be a lingering presence of animosity, which creates a distance, resulting in the lack of any type of communication.

No matter what nationality, people exude a certain degree of excitement and pleasure when someone from another country speaks or even attempts to speak their language. It shows that there was definitely an effort to fill the communication gap.

The students recognized in this book are some of many who fit the latter. They have the number one ingredient for success- Desire.

Like many others, they are faced with several issues that could prevent them from attending classes regularly or even at all. For example:

Transportation: Many times there is one vehicle in the family and that poses a problem because the spouse needs the vehicle to go to work. Additionally, sometimes the student does not have a driver's license.

Child Care: Sometimes the family cannot afford child care and does not initially know anyone who would assist them.

Jobs: Some students do get jobs commensurate with their level of knowledge of English, and at times, the hours can conflict with the class schedules.

Appointments: (legal/medical) These can occur quite often in certain cases.

Despite all these issues, reasons, excuses, challenges, these students find solutions and make the sacrifices necessary to achieve their goals. These sacrifices could be easily be replaced by "I cannot attend class because" but, some students realize that success warrants sacrifices and sacrifices equal success. Some people claim they are too old to study. Even as you get older, if you possess that spirit and desire, you can continue to learn,. Desire—it is a quality that is innate in everyone. It just depends on where you choose to direct it. The ages of these students range from 19-72

"Wisdom is priceless
Knowledge is powerful
Education is vital
Faith is monumental"

DSR

One student found time to volunteer in a hospital while she was attending class. She felt that in addition to the classes, being around people who spoke only English would also help. After volunteering for about eight months, she applied for a position in a local hospital and was hired. She still attends ESL classes.

In another instance, a student who did not want to discontinue her classes, sought advice from her instructor as to how she could continue her classes because her shift was changed and hours increased. Classes and schedules were arranged to accommodate her situation.

A student, who has never been late (more than a year's duration) had problems with her car. She woke up much earlier than usual and sat outside the car dealership until it opened at 0730 so she could be first in line. She was on time for her class.

Students also get together and organize rides when there is a problem with transportation, as referenced in one essay in the book.

Yet, another student, with a sixth grade education from her native country, by the way has never been late either, exhibits the qualities and actions of some students who are studying for a degree. Her inability to assist her daughter with her homework triggered her interest in taking ESL classes. Her approach toward learning, initiative, study habits and discipline would be an absolute wonder to any educator.

Another example of the desire to learn is the student whose son had a medical appointment. Before taking him to the appointment, the student stopped by the classroom with her son to turn in the homework, collect some notes and pick up the next day's assignment.

One soldier always found the time (time is something we can find) to attend class (even if he was late) before or after an appointment, after training or after duty.

The soldiers studying ESL are acutely aware of the importance of learning English. They realize that effective communication and comprehension are vital in the execution of not only the daily duties but the overall accomplishment of the mission. Even more aware are the non commissioned officers and the commanders who afford them the opportunity to fulfill this requirement without training interruption.

"Kudos" to these students! There are many more examples of students such as these, and they all should be applauded for their efforts.

Learning another language may not be mandatory, but it is definitely an asset, because maybe if we took the time to understand and learn about each other, effective communication will certainly surface and perhaps, just perhaps, the world can be a better place.

"If you go somewhere thinking you know
everything, you will learn nothing.
If you go somewhere wanting to learn everything,
you will learn something."

DSR

English As a Second Language; this is the meaning of ESL. You not only learn to read, speak and write in English, you take field trips and participate in lectures from guest speakers. I learned about different tenses and spelling. I also learned not to be ashamed of my mistakes or my accent. This class has strengthened my self confidence and also made it clear that it is completely okay when I make mistakes, because it's not my first language. You get to know other cultures and people whom you otherwise would have never met. For some, this class is the first step to establish contacts. You laugh together, get angry about English together and you help each other. It creates a community and sometimes friendships. This makes the homesickness much easier to endure.

Anne Buglowski
Germany

Englisch als zweite Sprache; dass bedeuter ESL ausgesprochen. Man lernt lessen, schreiben und die richtige Aussprache von Englisch. In diesen Kurs macht man Ausfluge und kleine Vortrage. Ich habe nicht nur die Zeitformen und Rechschreibung gelernt sondern auch mich nicht zu schamen uber meine Fehler oder meinenAkzent! Dieser Kurs hat mein selbst bewusst sehr gestarkt und auch klar gemacht das nicht vollkommen o.k. ist wenn ich fehler mache, weil es ist nicht meine Muttersprache. Man lacht zusammen, verflucht Englisch zusammen und hilft sich gegenseitig. Es entsteht eine Gemeinschaft vielleicht sogar ein Freundeskreis. So last sich das evtl. Heimweh viel leichter aushalten als allein.

Anne Buglowski
Germany

Krautroladen

Ingredients

one cabbage
half pound ground meat
salt
pepper
a little bit of garlic
one egg
one slice white bread
a little bit of milk
one onion
flour
paprika powder
veg. stock
string/ yarn

Directions

1. Soak white bread in a little bit of milk
2. Cut the onion in little pieces
3. Squeeze the milk out of the bread
4. Place the ground meat in a bowl, put salt, pepper, garlic, egg, bread, onion and mix
5. Boil the cabbage in salt water for around 5 minutes
6. Remove the leaves (they should not break), take a leaf and roll a little bit of meat in it
7. Take some string/ yarn and tie it (like a gift)
8. Put the Krautroladen in a pan, roast them until golden-brown, pour some water in the pan (the Krautroladen should be half in water)

9. Cook for around 30 -45 minutes
10. Remove the Krautroladen, add salt, pepper, paprika powder, veg. stock and simmer
11. Mix a little bit of flour with cold water and put it in the sauce ;boil for a few minutes.

Anne Buglowski
Germany

Zutaten

1 Weiskohl
500kg Hackfleisch
Salz
Pfefer
Knoblauch
1 Ei
1 ene Scheibe Weisbrot
Ein wenig Milch
1 Zweibel
Mehl
Paprikapulver
Bruhe
Schnurr

Zubereitung

1. dasWeisbrot in die milch einlegen fur ein paar Minuten
2. Zweibel in Wurfel schneiden
3. Hackfleisch in eine Schissel geben
4. Salz, pfeffer, Knoblauch, Ei, Zwiebeln und das ausgdrucckte brot zum Hackfleisch dazugeben
5. Alles gut durchkneten
6. Strink vom Kohl entfernen
7. Kohl fu c. 5 min. in salzwaser ziehen lassen
8. Vorsichtig die blatter vom Kohl losen
9. Das Hackfleisch in die Kohlblatter ein rollen
10. Mit schnurr zubinden (wie ein Geschenk)
11. Die Roladen anbraten

12. Dann mit Bruhe abloschen
13. Die Roladen ca. 30-45 min. kocheln
14. Roladen raus nehmen und die sose mit mehl andicken (kaltes wasser mit mehl mischen

I realize that I want to live and work in America; I must study English and attend ESL classes.

I want to be able to share my culture, but I cannot socialize with other students from other countries like Korea, Mexico, Puerto Rico, and Africa If I don't speak English.

There are so many cultures here at at the school. Learning English also builds self-confidence.

ESL helps me to get more experience. The first day I attended school, I did not understand anything about the homework that the teacher gave me to do.

After I attended school, I improved and I learned more about grammar, vocabulary, verbs, nouns, news, spelling words, writing, speaking, listening, and reading.

I want to learn English as a second language because it is important for me to speak, read, and write more than one language successfully.

Now I can understand more and I like my ESL class, and thank you teacher for helping me to correct all my mistakes.

Chantha Va
Cambodia

SAIFUN OR CH'A-ME SUR'E:

INGREDIENTS:

1 lb chicken
1 bag sai fun noodles
3/4 oz dry black mushrooms
3/4 oz dried bean curd sticks
3/4 oz dried fungus
2/3 oz dried lily flowers
2 carrots
1 onion
3 jalapeno
6 pieces garlic
3 green onion leaves
1/2 oz cilantro 1 tsp chicken flavor soup base mix (can)
1/2 tsp salt
2-1/2tsp sugar
1 tsp black pepper
2-1/2 tsp fish sauce
2-1/2 tsp soy sauce
2-1/2 tsp oyster sauce
1 cup of water
3 tsp of olive oil

METHOD:

1- heat oil in pan
2-put chopped garlic and stir until golden brown
3-add chicken and stir about 3 times.
4- put mushrooms, dried bean curd sticks, dried black fungus, dried lily
    flowers

5- add salt, sugar, black pepper, fish sauce, soy sauce, oyster sauce; boil
    water for about 15 minutes
6- put the noodles and stir until the noodles are cooked
7- put carrots, jalapeno, onion and stir for about 5 minutes
8- garnish with chopped green onion and cilantro.

Chantha Va
Cambodia

I have been taking ESL class for two years. I want to study English because I am living in the United States. If I don't know the language of the country I'm living in I might not end up enjoying it. If I know English well, I will be able to read books, magazines, newspapers and watch movies.

Knowing English will give me a chance to communicate with people from all over the world. What I like about ESL is that we have international students. I meet different people from different countries. And sometimes I learn about their cultures as well.

Although English is not easy, I will try my best. It is very hard since I don't have much education. I know learning English involves practicing and making mistakes. I know it takes a long time and sometimes I get mad but I need patience. I am learning new words, spelling, grammar and pronunciation in my class. I would like to thank my ESL teacher for what she does to help us to learn English.

Chong Blakely
Seoul, Korea

나는 2년동안 ESL 수업을 들어왔다. 내가 영어를 공부하고 싶은 이유는 내가 미국에 살고 있기 때문이다. 만약 내가 이 나라의 언어를 알지 못한다면 나는 이 나라를 충분히 즐길 수 없을지도 모른다. 만약 내가 영어를 잘 한다면 나는 책, 잡지, 신문들을 읽고 영화도 볼 수 있을 것이다.

이 수업에서 좋은 점은 외국 친구들을 만날 수 있다는 점이다. 나는 다른 나라에서 온 외국 친구들을 만난다. 그리고 가끔 나는 그들의 문화도 배운다.

영어를 배운다는 것은 어려운 일이지만 나는 최선을 다할 것이다. 나는 교육을 많이 받지 못해서 그것이 매우 어렵다. 영어를 배운다는 것은 연습과 실수를 포함하는 것이라는 것을 나는 안다. 시간이 많이 걸릴 것이고 가끔 화도 나겠지만 나에게 필요한 것은 끈기이다. 나는 수업시간에 새로운 단어, 철자, 문법, 발음 등을 배우고 있다.나는 영어를 배우려고 하는 우리를 도와주고 있는 우리 선생님에게 감사하다고 말하고 싶다.

정 블레이클리
서울, 대한민국

Stewed Kalbi (Beef short ribs)

Ingredients:

2-3 pounds of Kalbi (beef short ribs), trimmed
10 chestnuts, peeled (optional)
7 daikon radish, chopped
½ carrot, chopped
8 dates or jujube (optional)
Pine nuts
15 gingko nuts, unshelled (optional)
To boil the meat:
1 green onion
Black pepper
4 cloves of garlic
1 ginger
Enough water to cover the meat
Sauce: 5 tsp soy sauce, 2 tsp sugar, 3 tsp rice wine, 2 tsp minced garlic,
     1/2cup pear juice, 1/2 onion puree, 2 tsp sesame oil, 1 tsp corn syrup,
     black pepper

Directions:

1. Remove fat from the meat, and blanch meat in cold water for about an hour.
2. Combine the meat, green onion, garlic, ginger, black pepper and pour enough water to cover the beef in the same pan.
3. Bring to a boil on medium high heat until the beef is half-way cooked.
4. Remove the beef in a bowl and drain the water using paper towels for clean broth and save it.
5. Combine soy sauce, sugar, rice wine, minced garlic, pear juice, onion puree.
6. Combine the meat, broth, and sauce in a large pan.

7. Cook over low-medium heat about 20-30 minutes or until the meat becomes tender.
8. When half-way cooked, add dates, chestnuts, daikon radish and carrot to the meat.
9. Add black pepper, sesame oil, corn syrup, gingko nuts, and pine nuts and stir.
10. Serve with steamed rice.

Chong Blakely
Seoul, Korea

갈비찜

〈재료〉

갈비 2-3 파운드
대파잎 1대
후주
통마늘 4쪽
생강 1쪽
물잠길정도
밤10개
대추 8개
은행 15개,
잣약간
무 7 토막
당근 1/2 개
양념장: 간장 5큰술, 설탕2큰술, 청주 3큰술, 다진마늘 2큰술, 배즙 1/2개분,
　　양파즙 1/2개분, 후추약간, 참기름 2큰술, 물엿 1큰술

〈만드는법〉

1. 토막낸갈비는기름을떼어내고물에 1시간정도담가두어핏물을뺀다.
2. 갈비가잠길정도의물을붓고생강, 마늘,대파, 통후추를넣고갈비가 1/2
   정도익을정도까지삶는다.
3. 삶아진갈비는꺼내고국물은거름종이에받혀걸러낸다.
4. 고명의대추는깨끗이씻고, 밤은껍질을벗긴다.
5. 무, 당근은밤크기로모서리를동글동글하게다듬어준다.
6. 은행은겉껍질을벗겨팬에식용유를두르고소금을약간넣고볶
   아껍질을벗긴다.
7. 양념장을만든다.후추, 참기름, 물엿은나중에넣는다.

8. 팬에 삶아진 갈비와 걸러낸 갈비 국물,
   양념장을 넣고 갈비가 부드러울 때까지 끓인다.
9. 중간에 은행, 잣을 뺀 고명을 넣고 갈비와 함께 졸인다.
10. 국물이 촉촉하게 남고 갈비가 부드러워지면 마지막으로 후추, 참기름,
    물엿을 넣고 뒤적이면서 은행과 잣을 섞어낸다.

I have been attending ESL class for about six months. I am totally satisfied with my class. I am lucky to have a good teacher. I think her teaching style is very good for me.

Everybody knows, learning a language is not easy and it is hard to notice an improvement, but I learned a lot and I can feel that I have improved in my English.

Firstly, each day we are assigned to bring a news story and read it in front of class. It was hard for me. I could not understand my classmates' accent, because I was used to Korean style English which I learned from Korean teachers, and it was my first experience with real foreigners except my husband. We meet many people with different accents while we live in America, therefore this is a good way to be familiar with each other's accents.

Moreover, the homework improves my reading skills and my intellectual capacity, because I have to read many news articles to pick an appropriate one for presentation.

Secondly, my teacher emphasizes the grammar part.

At first, I did not think grammar is important, because even native Americans often use poor grammar. I think the young generation destroys grammar these days. I wanted to learn the speaking and listening part more. I thought that those would be more helpful to get a job later. But because of this class, I realized I was wrong. Grammar is an important part because in the beginning, if I use bad grammar, it will be difficult to correct later on. So I think I am lucky. I am building a good foundation now.

Thirdly, she helps me to have self-confidence.

I was a very shy student. I was embarrassed to raise my hand or say something during classes, even if I knew the right answers. Sometimes, I still hesitate to do something but I am learning to speak up and express myself in the class.

The ESL class has helped me with my English, my self-confidence and understanding others. I never expected that a free English class would be of such of a high quality education?

Now, I've started a volunteer job and finally I have a job offer from there. I could not have been here without my teacher. I know, actually this essay should be about the ESL class, but I really want to mention about it. There are many schools and many teachers. But she is very special to me. She is an excellent teacher, very passionate and has wonderful patience with her students.

I am happy to be learning English from her and growing with my classmates.

Hyang Kwon
Dongducheon, Korea

나는 ESL 수업을 들은 지 반년 정도 된 학생이다. 나는 이 수업에 대해 200% 만족한다. Ramos 선생님을 만난 건 나에게 행운이라 할 수 있다. 그녀의 수업 방식은 나에게 딱 맞는 스타일이다.

모든 사람들이 알다시피 다른 언어를 배운다는 것은 결코 쉬운 일이 아님을, 그리고 향상되어 가고 있음을 자각하기란 매우 어려운 일이다. 그럼에도 불구하고 나는 여기서 정말 많은 것을 배웠고 내가 향상되어가고 있음을 분명히 느낄 수 있다. 이제 나는 내가 이 수업을 들으며 느꼈던 내 경험들과 또 여기서 무엇을 배웠는지를 나누고 싶다.

첫 번째로, 우리는 매일 뉴스를 읽고 카피해서 학교로 가져와서 발표해야 하는 과제가 있다. 한국인이 가르치는 한국인 방식의 영어에 익숙해져 있던 나에게, 또한 진짜 외국인들과 대면하는 것은 남편을 제외하고는 처음이었던 터라 다른 학생들의 억양과 발음을 알아듣고 이해하기란 굉장히 어려운 일이었다. 우리는 미국에 살면서 많은 다양한 억양을 가진 사람들을 만나게 된다. 그러므로 이것은 각자 다른 억양들에 익숙해지기 위한 매우 좋은 훈련방법이라 할 수 있다. 또한 발표를 위해 적합한 기사를 고르기 위해서 많은 뉴스를 읽어야 하므로 이 숙제는 나의 영어 읽기 능력뿐만 아니라 지적 능력을 향상시키는 효과가 있었다.

두 번째로, Ramos 선생님은 문법을 매우 강조하는 편이다.
처음에는 나는 문법이 그리 중요하다고 생각하지 않았다. 요즘에는 오리지널 미국 사람조차도 틀린 문법을 사용하고 젊은 세대들은 문법을 파괴하기도 하기 때문이다. 나는 말하기와 듣기를 더 배우고 싶었다. 그리고 나는 그것들이 나중에 내가 직장을 가지는데 더 도움이 될 것이라 생각했다. 그러나 그것은 잘못된 생각이었다. 문법은 처음 배울 때 가장 중요한 부분이다. 만약 처음부터 잘못된 습관이 들어지면 나중에 고치기는 더 어렵기 때문이다. 좋은 기초를 쌓아 갈 수 있어 다행이라 생각한다.

세 번째로, 그녀는 내가 자신감을 찾는데 큰 도움이 되었다.
나는 수줍음이 많은 편이라 학교 생활을 하는 동안, 내가 설사 정답을 알고 있다 할 지라도 한번도 손을 들고 발표를 한다거나 내 의견을 피력해본 적이 없었다.
때때로 나는 여전히 무엇을 할 때 주저하는 경향이 아직은 있지만, 수업을 통해 내 목소리를 내고 내 의견을 표현하는 법을 배우고 있다.

ESL 수업은 내가 영어를 배우고 다른 사람들을 이해하며 내가 자신감을 찾는데 많은 도움을 주었다. 무료로 하는 수업에서 이렇게 양질의 수업을 들을 수 있게 되리라곤 전혀 기대하지 못했던 바다.

　　지금 나는 자원 봉사도 시작했고 거기에서 고용제의도 받았다.

　　아마 Ramos선생님이 없었다면 나는 오늘 이 자리까지 올 수 없었을 것이다.

　　수업에 관한 에세이를 써야 하는 것을 알지만 내가 꼭 언급하고 싶은 것이 있다.

　　세상에는 많은 학교도 있고 많은 선생님도 있지만 그녀는 내게 특별하다. 그녀는 정말 훌륭한 선생님이고 열정이 넘치며 대단한 인내로 우리를 가르친다.

　　나는 Ramos 선생님에게 영어를 배우는 것과 우리 반 친구들과 함께 커나가는 것이 즐겁다.

Hyang Kwon

Sik-Hye

Sik-hye is a Korean traditional beverage made with malt which is a kind of fermented rice punch and a healthy drink.

Ingredients

1 cup malt
1 cup white sugar
1 cup rice
6 cups water
1 piece (small size) ginger

Directions

1. Pour malt into cold water, knead for 3-5 minutes.
2. Strain through a cloth or colander.
3. Discard the strained malt and keep the malt water 2-3 hours at room temperature.
4. Cook rice with 1/4 less water than normal in a rice cooker. Allow to cool or rinse with cold tap water.
5. After 2-3 hours, carefully pour the top, clear part of the malt water into the rice cooker with cooked rice and sugar. Do not allow dregs of malt in.
6. Set the rice cooker on a warm setting for 4-6 hours.
7. Transfer it to another pot and boil again for 30 minutes, to avoid pot boiling over.
8. Add ginger, more sugar or more water to taste.
9. Transfer drink to pitcher or glasses and cool it in a refrigerator.

Hyang Kwon
Dongducheon, Korea

식혜

식혜는 한국에서 인기 있는 엿기름으로 만든 일종의 쌀 발효 건강 음료이다.

〈재료〉

엿기름 1컵
백설탕 1컵
쌀 1컵
물 6 컵
생강 작은 것 1쪽

〈만드는 법〉

1. 엿기름을 찬 물에 넣고 3-5분동안 잘 치대어준다.
2. 천이나 가는 체를 이용하여 걸러준다.
3. 걸러진 엿기름 찌꺼기는 버리고, 걸러진 엿기름 물을 상온에 2-3 시간 정도 놓아둔다.
4. 한편 밥통에 밥을 짓되 평소보다 물을 조금 적게 하여 밥을 고슬고슬하게 짓는다. 밥이 다 되면 식혀두거나 찬 물로 헹궈둔다.
5. 2-3 시간이 지나면 상온에 놓아둔 엿기름 물을 조심스럽게 맑은 물만 따라내어 준비한 밥과 설탕과 함께 밥통에 넣는다. 이때 앙금이 같이 들어가지 않게 주의한다.
6. 전기 밥통을 보온으로 셋팅한 후 4-6 시간 정도 둔다.
7. 준비된 과정이 모두 끝나면 이것을 모두 큰 냄비에 옮겨 담고 넘치지 않도록 주의하면서 가스 불에서 30분 정도 다시 끓여준다.
8. 기호에 따라 생강을 넣거나 설탕이나 물을 더 첨가하여도 좋다.
9. 유리병이나 용기에 옮겨 담은 후 냉장고에서 차게 보관하고 시원할 때 흔들어서 마신다.

Hyang Kwon

I started my ESL class, in May 2012, in Central Texas College, and I can say that English classes changed my life. During this year I improved my communication. I started to communicate with others, using short sentences and understanding more, and I learn a lot of vocabulary.

I go to the Doctor's office and try to explain my symptoms. Being able to go to the market and ask about products and find them makes me feel good. Now, I like to go to the movies because I can understand some dialogues and I can get the general idea. I am still learning and I would like to continue my ESL classes in Central Texas College.

Irma Hernandez
Colombia

Como las Clases de Ingles Cambiaron mi Vida

Yo llegue de Colombia en Abril 5/2012. Yo hablo español y no tengo experiencia aprendiendo el idioma Ingles. Yo comencé mi clase de ESOL en Mayo 2012 en Central Texas College. Continué desde Agosto 2012 y puedo decir que las clases de Ingles cambiaron mi vida. Durante este año yo mejore mi comunicación:

Yo empecé a comunicarme con las demás personas usando frases cortas y entendiendo mas. Yo aprendí mucho vocabulario. Yo fui al consultorio médico e intente explicar mis síntomas. Yo puedo preguntar acerca de los productos en el supermercado. Yo entiendo y canto las canciones de mi iglesia.

Me gusta ir al cine y ahora entiendo algunos diálogos y la idea general.

Yo estoy en el proceso de aprender y me gusta continuar mis clases en Central Texas College.

Irma Hernandez
Bogota, Colombia

Chocolate Santafereno

Ingredients.

    4 chocolate tablets.
    6 cups of milk
    Almojabanas

Preparation

1) Place the milk and the chocolate pieces in a small pot with high sides over medium heat.
2) Slowly stir the chocolate to help it dissolver in the milk.
3) Bring to a boil three times.
4) Lower the heat.
5) Quickly beat the mixture to create a foamy top.
6) Serves six

Irma Hernandez
Bogota, Colombia

Chocolate Santafereno

Ingredientes

4 pastillas de chocolate
6 tasas de leche
Almojábanas.

Preparation

1. En una olleta se echa la leche y el chocolate.
2. Se pone a hervir a fuego mediano.
3. Con un monilinillo se empieza a batir para disolver el chocolate.
4. Se deja hervir tres veces.
5. Se bate antes de servir para que forme una espesa espuma.
6. Se sirve para seis personas.

ESL is an unbelievable help for me. I felt lost after my arrival in the USA. I had no knowledge of English and I knew no one. I tried to teach myself but was unsuccessful. A radical change happened after I started ESL. My abilities with the English language improved drastically, for which I have the competent and extremely patient teacher to thank. In her personification, I found what I was looking for in a teacher; someone who is very demanding of her students, but at the same time offers an excellent classroom environment. In class, I received answers to all my questions, and they were not few. They cover not only English grammar and pronunciation, but normal items from everyday life. Every immigrant knows what I am saying. An added benefit I have received from ESL is the many people from different countries and cultures I have met. I have established a lot of friendships that mean a lot to me. I recommend that all immigrants who want to make America their home attend ESL classes.

Izabela Quinn
Czech Republic

ESL je pre mna neopisatelna pomoc.

Po mojom prichode do USA som sa citila byt stratena. Neovladala som tunajsi jazyk a nepoznala som tu nikoho. Snazila som sa ucit anglictinu ako samouk, ale bezuspesne.

Radikalny obrat nastal ked som zacala chodit do ESL. Moje jazykove znalosti sa podstatne zlepsili vdaka mojej kompetentnej a neuveritelne trpezlivej ucitelke. V jej osobe som nasla presne to co som hladala. Niekoho kto je narocny na studentov, ale zaroven im poskytuje vzorovu vyucbu.

V skole dostavam odpoved na vsetky moje otazky—a tych nie je malo. Netykaju sa iba gramatiky a vyslovnosti, ale aj normalneho bezneho zivota. Kazdy privandrovalec vie o com pisem.

Co ma pre mna nezaplatitelnu hodnotu je to, ze v ESl som spoznala mnoho ludi z roznych krajin sveta. Nadviazala som tu priatelstva ktore mi znamenaju velmi vela.

Odporucam kazdemu cudzincovi ktory sa chce udomacnit v Amerike, studovat v ESL.

Izabela Quinn
Slovak Republic

Segedin Goulash (Segedínsky guláš)

A dish you'll find in most Slovak restaurants, usually served with dumplings.

Ingredients:

- Pork shoulder—1.5 lbs (cubed)
- Sauerkraut—1 lb
- Onion—1 medium
- Flour—3 tablespoons (tbsp)
- Sour cream—1 cup
- Butter
- Salt, paprika, black pepper, caraway seed

Instructions:

1. Cut onion into very small pieces and brown it in butter.
2. Add pieces of pork, 1 teaspoon of paprika, half teaspoon of caraway seeds, black pepper and salt.
3. Fry it (stirring all the time) until pork is cooked on all sides.
4. When pork is ready, add sauerkraut and some water, so the mixture is fully covered.
5. Cook covered for 70-80 minutes. If necessary, add more water and simmer it sometimes.
6. To thicken the sauce, brown 3 tbsp of flour on melted butter and mix it into the stew.
7. Stir in sour cream and let it boil for a few minutes.

Izabela Quin
Czech Republic

Segedinsky gulas

Potrebujeme:

- Bravcove plece—750 g
- Kyslu kapustu -250 g
- Cibulu—stredne velku
- Muku—3 polievkove lyzice
- Kyslu smotanu—1 salku
- Maslo
- Sol, papriku, cierne korenie, kmin

Navod na pripravu:

1. Cibulu pokrajame na velmi male kusky a oprazime ju na masle
2. Pridame kusky masa, 1 cajovu lyzicku papriky, polovicu cajovej lyzicky kminu, cierneho korenia a soli
3. Oprazime (za staleho miesania) zo vsetkych stran
4. K masu pridame kapustu, podlejeme vodou
5. Prikryte dusime 70-80 minut. Podla potreby dolejeme vodu, obcas premiesame
6. Na zahustenie pripravime zaprazku z 3 lyzic muky a masla a zamiesame k masu a kapuste
7. Pridame kyslu smotanu a nechame zovriet.

Servirujeme s knedlou.

The reason I am taking ESL is to improve my English and also to have more opportunities for employment and communicate better with my family and others. My oldest son does not speak Spanish. He understands a lot, but he does not speak it. Also, I can help with their homework, and when I have a medical appointment I don't have to take my husband to translate for me. I have always wanted to learn English because it can help me in my future. At the end of this ESL course, I would like to read better and at the same time work with my writing in English. Also, I would like to pronounce words better and improve my English vocabulary.

Janet Martinez
Puerto Rico

La razon en el cual estoy cojiendo ESL espara mejorar mi Ingles, y tambien tener mas oportunidades para empleo Communicarme mejor con mi familia y otros. Mi hijo mayor no habla Espanol, el entiende mucho pero no lo habla. Yo tambien le puedo ayudar en sustareas y cuando yo tenga unacitamedica, no tender que llevarme a mi esposo paraque me tradusca. yo siempre he queridoaprender el idioma del Ingles, porque me puedeayudar en mi futuro. Y quisiera que al final de este curso de ESL, me gustaria leer mejor y a la vestra bajar con mi escritura en Ingles. Tambien me gustaria pronunciar las palabras mejor y a la vez superar mi vocabulario en Ingles.

Janet Martinez
Puerto Rico

Rice With Green Pigeon Peas

Ingredients :

2 cups of long grain rice
3 cups of water
2 tbs of sofrito (a mixture of onions, peppers, cilantro, garlic)
2 cans of green pigeon peas
1 pk. of sazon goya coriander and annatto
2 tbs of oil
2 tbs of salt
5 oz of ham or sausage
1 pimiento (diced)

Directions

1. Mix the green pigeon peas in a saucepan with oil, sofrito, ham or sausage, diced pimientos, sazon goya coriander and annatto
2. Add water and bring to a boil
3. Add rice and salt
4. Stir and cover
5. Simmer until the rice is cooked
6. Stir and serve

Janet Martinez
Puerto Rico

Arroz con Gandules

Ingredientes :

2 tazas de arroz grano largo
3 tazasde agua
2 cucharadas de sofrito
1 cucharada de aceite
2 cucharaditas de sal
2 potes dev gandules
5 onzas de hamon o' sausage
1 pimiento morrones
1 sobrecito de sazon goya cilantro y achote

Preparacion :

1. Mescle los gandules en un cardero con aceite, sofrito, hamon o'sausage, pimientos morrones, sazon con achote.
2. Anadele el agua asta que hierba
3. Anadale el arroz y la sal
4. Mueva el arroz y tape el caldero
5. Cocine a fuego lento hasta que el arroz este seco
6. Mueva y sirve

Janet Martinez
Puerto Rico

My "ESL" class has been the key in achieving my goal to speak, understand and write proper English. Through English classes I have opened many doors in my life. It has made me feel more secure when I express myself and be independent.

The class has given me the opportunity to participate and have debates with classmates. Through this program, students gain a lot of knowledge.

In English class I learned about the rules, exceptions and the correct way of writing, listening and speaking English. In my opinion, the "ESL" class has been very important in learning. Every day that I have the opportunity to be present in class, I learn something new and that makes me more motivated to continue attending and getting more knowledge.

Jasmarin Montes González
Añasco, Puerto Rico

Mi clase de "ESL" ha sido una herramienta clave para lograr mi objetivo de hablar, entender y escribir inglés adecuadamente. Las clases de inglés me han permitido abrir muchas puertas en mi vida. Me ha hecho que me sienta más segura a la hora de comunicarme y de poder ser independiente.

La clase me ha dado la oportunidad de participar y de tener debates con compañeros de clase. El programa tiene un amplio y alto contenido de materiales y conocimiento para ofrecer a los estudiantes. A través de este programa, los estudiantes obtenemos una gran cantidad de conocimiento.

En las clases de inglés he aprendido acerca de las reglas, excepciones y la forma correcta de escribir, escuchar y hablar el inglés. En mi opinión, la clase de "ESL" ha sido muy importanteen mi aprendizaje. Cada día que tengo la oportunidad de estar presente en la clase, aprendo algo nuevo y eso hace que me motive más para seguir asistiendo y seguir adquiriendo conocimiento.

Cheese Flan

Ingredients:

- 1 can evaporated milk (12oz)
- 1 can condensed milk (14oz)
- 4 eggs (large)
- 1 cream cheese (8oz, a box)
- 1 1/2 cup sugar
- 1 tsp water

Procedure:

1. Mix all ingredients, except the water and the sugar, in a blender.
2. Preheat the oven to 350F degrees.
3. Heat the sugar and water over medium heat, until it has a light brown color
4. Pour the caramel into the mold and cover the entire mold.
5. Pour the mixture into the flan mold.
6. Put the mold with the mixture in a water bath, the water can't come inside the mixture
7. Put into the oven for 35-45 minutes or until cooked.
8. Check completion by placing small knife or a toothpick in the center of the flan; if it comes relatively clean that means it's ready.
9. Serve cold
10. Serves 6-8

Jasmarín Montes González
Añasco, Puerto Rico

Flan De Queso

Ingredientes:

- 1 lata de leche evaporada (12oz)
- 1 lata de leche condensada (14oz)
- 4 huevos grandes (5 pequeños)
- 1 caja de queso crema (8oz)
- 1 cucharadita de vainilla
- 1 1/2 taza de azúcar
- 1 cucharada de agua

Procedimiento:

1. Mezclar todos los ingredientes, excepto el agua y el azúcar, en la licuadora.
2. Precalentar el horno a 350F grados.
3. Colocar el agua con el azúcar en una sartén en la estufa, mezclar hasta que la azúcar se caramelice (debe verse con un color marrón claro).
4. Colocar el caramelo en el molde, cubrir completo hasta arriba con el caramelo.
5. Colocar la mezcla de todos los ingredientes en el molde.
6. Colocar el molde en baño de maría, el agua no debe tocar la mezcla,
7. Poner dentro de horno durante 35-45 minutos o hasta que esté cocido.
8. Verifica si esta hecho colocando un cuchillo pequeño o un palillo de diente en el centro del flan, si éste sale casi limpio es que está listo.
9. Servir frío.
10. Porcion:6-8

Jasmarín Montes González
Añasco, Puerto Rico

When I arrived to Texas from Puerto Rico I only spoke basic English, but I didn't know to speak correctly. I was terrified to say something in English because I thought that if I said something wrong people would laugh about it or wouldn't understand me. When I started taking ESL classes everything was different, I have been taking classes for six months and I learned about grammar and how to use it correctly. I feel more confident when speaking English. Also I learned about verbs, subject, the past tense and how to speak in complete sentences. I learned how to make questions correctly. I improved my vocabulary and I feel much better, I think that I learned a lot in those months. I know that I need to learn more. I am very confident with all that I learned.

Johanna Jimenez Frias
Dominican Republic

A mi llegada a texas desde puerto rico yo solo hablaba lo basico del ingles pero no sabia como hablarlo correctamente, tenia miedo de pronuciar una palabra en ingles por que pensaba que si cometia errores al hablarlo las personas se reirian de mi cuando me escucharan hablarlo, o que no me entendieran, pero cuando comenze a tomar las clases de esl todo es diferente, llevo 6 meses tomando clases y he aprendido bastante, he aprendido sobre gramatica, como usarla correctamente, he aprendido a perder el miedo cuando lo hablo, tambien sobre los verbos, subjetos y etc, tambien he aprendido como hablar en presente o pasado, como hablar con oraciones completas, hacer preguntas correctamente, he aprendido muchas palabras nuevas, me siento mucho mejor, cre que he aprendido bastante en los meses que llevo tomando las clases, se qu todavia me faltamucho por aprender, pero estoy muy conforme por lo que he logrado hasta ahora y todo lo que he aprendido en esl class.

Johanna Jiminez Frias
Dominican Republic

Mangu

INGREDIENTS:

1. 5 PLANTAINS OR MORE
2. SALT TO TASTE
3. BUTTER

TO MAKE ONION GARNISH

2 large onions
2 tbsp of olive oil
1tbsp of fruit vinegar
salt to taste

Method:

1. Peel the plantains and cut into 8 small pieces.
2. Boil the plantains and add salt to taste.
3. Take the plantains out of the water and mash them with a fork until they are very soft.
4. Add butter and mix.
5. Add water cold and keep mashing and mixing until it is very smooth.

Method for the onions:

1. Heat a tablespoon of oil in pan
2. Add onions and cook until they become transparent
3. Add vinegar and salt to taste.
4. Garnish mangu with the onions and serve.
- You can combine with salami or scrambled eggs and enjoy.

Johanna Jiminez Frias
Dominican Republic

ingredientes:

1. 5 platanos o mas.
2. sal al gusto.
3. mantequilla al gusto.

ingredientes para preparar la cebolla:

1. 2 cd de aceite de oliva.
2. 2 cebollas rojas grande.
3. lcd de vinagre de fruta.
4. sal al gusto

instrucciones:

1. pelar los platanos y cortarlos en 8 pedazos pequeños.
2. poner a hervir los platanos con sal al gusto.
3. cuando los platanos esten listo, sacar los platanos del agua y majar con un tenedor hasta que no queden grumos.
4. despues agrega la mantequilla y mezclar.
5. agrega un poco de agua fria y mas mantequilla si es necesario, mantener mezclando todo hasta que quede como un pure sin grumos.

Ingredientes para la cebolla:

1. calentar aceite en un sarten.
2. despues que el aceite caliente agrega la cebolla hasta que la cebolla se torne transparente.
3. despues agrega el vinagre y sal al gusto.
4. Combina la cebolla con el mangu y sirve.

*Puedes Acompañar El Mangu Con Huevo O Salami

When I started ESL classes three years ago my main purpose was to increase my reading comprehension and my writing skills.

Since September of 2012 the ESL class I am currently attending has been very helpful in obtaining my goals. Going to class four days is much better than the two day classes I went to before.

Unlike many younger students who may have come to this country, I have been here a while, and I am looking for personal accomplishments.

My comprehension has improved a great deal. I understand what I am reading and I am able to ask questions when I do not understand what I have read.

I have a much better understanding of news, and how to ask and answer questions, verbally and in writing. I know there is much more to learn and I want to continue to grow and become more confident and to accomplish this, I will continue my ESL studies.

Kim Croker
Korea

내가 3년전 ESL 과정을 시작했을 때, 나의 목표는 읽기와 쓰기 능력을 향상시키는 것이었다.

2012년 9월부터 지금까지 ESL 수업에서 공부한 것들은 내 목표를 이루는데 매우 많은 도움이 되어 주었다. 지금 일주일에 4일 다니는 이 수업은 이전에 다녔던 일주일에 이틀만 다니면 되는 학교보다 훨씬 더 도움이 된다.

최근에 이 나라로 오게 된 많은 젊은 학생들과는 달리 나는 여기에 출석하는 동안 내 개인적인 성취감을 느낄 수 있게 되길 기대한다.

이해 능력이 향상된 것은 내게 매우 커다란 의미를 가져다 준다. 나는 내가 읽은 것을 이해 할 수 있고 읽은 것을 이해하지 못할 때는 물어 볼 수 있게 되었다.

나는 뉴스를 이해하는 게 훨씬 나아졌고 또 글을 쓸 때나 말을 할 때 질문하는 법과 또 질문에 어떻게 답해야 하는지 잘 알게 되었다. 나는 더 배워야 하는 것이 아직 많이 남아있다. 나는 ESL 수업을 계속 들을 것이며 계속 더 성장해서 자신감을 갖고 내 목표들을 성취하기를 원한다.

크로커 김
대한민국

Quick Korean Kimchi

INGREDIENTS:

1—large Chinese cabbage
½ cup—regular table salt
2—garlic cloves
2—green onions
1 tablespoon—sugar
2 tablespoon—sesame seeds
2 tablespoons—red pepper powder

DIRECTIONS:

1. Slice cabbage lengthwise into four pieces; place cabbage in a large mixing bowl.
2. Pour ½ cup of salt over cabbage, then pour a cup of water over cabbage, set aside and let stand for half an hour.
3. Place cabbage in a colander and rinse well with cold water; when fully drained, remove from colander and cut into small pieces and place it back in mixing bowl.
4. Cut green onions into small pieces and add to cabbage; crush garlic cloves and add to bowl along with 1 tablespoon of sugar, 2 tablespoons of sesame seeds and 2 tablespoons of red pepper powder.
5. Using hands or salad utensils thoroughly mix all ingredients; when finished Kimchi is ready to serve.

Kim Croker
Korea

겉절이 김치

재료

중국배추 1단
소금 1/2 컵
마늘 2 쪽
파 2단
설탕 1스푼
참깨 2 스푼
고추가루 2 스푼

조리방법

1. 배추를 4등분하여 큰 그릇에 담아 준비한다.
2. 소금 1/2컵과 물을 넣어 만든 소금물로 위의 배추를 30분 정도 절여준다.
3. 절여진 배추는 찬 물로 잘 헹구고 체에 받쳐 물기를 뺀 후 먹기 좋은 크기로 잘라 다시 큰 믹싱 볼에 담는다.
4. 작은 크기로 자른 파, 마늘 찧은 것, 설탕, 참깨, 고추가루를 넣어준다.
5. 손이나 샐러드용 집게를 사용하여 잘 버무려준다.

April 5, 2012 was my first day into the ESL class. I was presented to a very disciplined and lovely teacher. On that day the first thing I did was fill out the school registration form. After that the teacher asked me to present myself to the class, and the students in the class, also presented themselves to me one by one.

Even though we came from different countries and had different school levels, we were learning together without any complications.

The ESL class helped me a lot to improve my English in different areas. My speaking improved through talking with my schoolmates and the teacher; also my reading and writing improved. We wrote many essays about movies and holidays. This class helped me to do research on the internet and in the newspaper. Twice a week, we brought news to the class and read it in front of our classmates. I learned many words and their pronunciation. We were asked to bring one new word from the dictionary every day which increased my vocabulary. I also improved my listening skills, because if you don't listen well you cannot do the spelling words.

My teacher helps me so much. She calls me many times to answer questions, and this encourages me to prepare myself to learn more at home before coming to school. We did our homework with discipline. If you don't do the home work you lose your ESL Dollars. We work individually, but sometimes as a team. She put all the class together as a family and we had great wisdom. She told us it is never too late to learn if you have desire, determination and dedication.

My classmates and my teacher love me as a blood sister' and daughter'. When I was pregnant they assisted me a lot. When my turn came to do my class responsibility duties, they cleaned the board, and picked up the books for me. One month before my pregnancy due date, they had a baby shower for me with many beautiful gifts.

In conclusion, the class helped me a lot in many ways, especially the atmosphere of caring impressed me so much. I can never forget my classmates especially Chantha. She gives me a ride to class every time when my husband is training.

I recommend this ESL class to everyone who wants to learn English as a Second Language. There will be no regrets.

Lydia Lasisi
Togo, Africa

LE 5, Avril 2012 était mon premier jour dans la classe d'ESL. Je me fus présenté à l'institutrice, une institutrice très aimable et disciplinée. La première chose que j'avais fait ce jour, c'était de remplir la fiche de registre. Après cela la maitresse m'a demandé de me présentera la classe, tous les élèves qui étaient dans la classe s'étaient présentés à moi un a un.

Malgré que nous venions de différents pays et que nous avions des niveaux scolaires différents, nous apprenions ensemble sans aucun complexe.

La classe d'ESL m'a beaucoup aide à améliorer mon anglais sur plusieurs plans. Le fait de parler avec mes camarades et ma maitresse a amélioré mon parle; ma lecture et la rédaction aussi s'étaient améliorées. Nous avions rédigé plusieurs rédactions sur des films et des jours de fêtes. Cette classe m'a aidé à faire des recherches sur l'internet et dans les journaux ; nous apportions deux fois par semaines des nouvelles que nous lisions devant la classe, j'avais appris plusieurs mots et leurs prononciations, nous amenions tous les jours, dans le dictionnaire un mot, dont nous ne connaissions pas le sens. Si tu n'écoutes pas bien tu ne pourras pas faire la dictée, cela a fait que j'ai amélioré mon entendement.

M'avais beaucoup aidée, elle m'appelé chaque temps pour répondre à des questions; cela m'avais encouragé a bien se préparer à la maison avant de venir à l'école. Nous faisions nos devoirs de maison avec discipline, si tu ne fais pas ton devoir de maison, tu perds ton ESL Dollars. Nous travaillions individuellement, et parfois en groupe. Elle a regroupe la classe ensemble comme une famille, avec une grande sagesse, et elle nous disait qu'il n'a jamais trop tard pour apprendre, si tu as le désire, et la détermination.

Mes camarades et ma maitresse m'aimaient comme une sœur de même sang et comme une fille. Quand j'étais enceinte, lorsque mon tour de responsabilité scolaire venait, la classe m'assistait à nettoyer le tableau et à ramasser les livres. Un mois avant mon accouchement la classe avait fêté l'arrivée de mon bébé, appelé "baby show er" en m'offrant de jolies cadeaux.

EN conclusion, la classe m'avait aidé en divers manières. L'atmosphère d'amour qui régnait m'avait beaucoup impressionne. Je n'oublierais jamais Chantal, une amie qui venait me prendre avec sa voiture quand mon mari n'est pas à la maison.

Je recommande cette ESL classe à celui qui veut apprendre l'anglais comme une seconde langue. Vous ne vont pas regret.

Lydia Lasisi (Balogun)
Togo, Afrique

INGREDIENTS:

Red pepper
Tomato paste
Tomato sauce
onion
salt
oil
maggi (seasoning),
farina of corn,
chicken broth,
fried chicken.

DIRECTIONS

1. Pour oil into the saucepan for 2 minutes and add a small piece of onion to change the oil odour,
2. Add 3 teaspoons of tomato paste (2 minutes)
3. Add tomato sauce, pepper, salt, magi seasoning and stir to make a stew(3 minutes)
4. Add 2 cups of water, let it boil for 5 minutes
5. Pour the farina of corn and stir to make paste
6. Serves two people
7. Garnish it with diced onions, pepper, diced tomatoes and fried chicken.

Nom: EJEKOUME

INGREDIENTS:

Piment
patetomate
saucetomate
oignon
sel
huile
maggi cube
farine de mais
bouillon de poulet
pouletfrite

INSTRUCTION DE CUISINE

1. Mets la casserole sur leréchaud et allume le feu, verser de l'huile dans la casserole pour 2 minutes et ajouter un peu d'oignions coupe en des pour changer l'odeur de l'huile
2. Après une minute il faut ajouter 3 cuilleresde pate de tomate de dans, et ajouter
3. Après 2 minutes, la sauce detomate en boite, et le piment rouge, le sel, maggicube, remuer le tout pour en faire unesauce
4. Apres 3 minutes ajouter 0.5 litre d'eau, laisser le tout bouillit pour 5minutes
5. Verser la farine de mais dans la sauce et remuer pour faire lapaste de mais appel "EJEKOUME", la cuison est finie
6. le plat est pres pour deux personnes
7. Tugarnis le tout avec de l'oignon en des, poivron, tomates coupe en des et du poulet frite

When I started this class I knew what E S L means. E= English, S= Second, L= language.

I am learning how to write English with the right grammar and speak correctly. Also I am learning new vocabulary and how to pronounce words. I see so many different cultures in E S L class, and all my classmates are from different countries. One of my friends is from china, some are from Europe, some are from Africa and many other countries . . .

We don't just learn about English, but we learn how to live in America. And we learn how to communicate with other people. I feel really lucky that I had an opportunity to come to study in an E S L class. I Learn so many things and get so much information in my E S L class, and now I can speak in English a little bit better with other people.

AmphonnalyThamavongsa
Vientiane Laos

ຄວາມຮູ້ສຶກກ່ຽວກັບ E S L

ແຕ່ກ່ອນຂ້ອຍເອງບໍ່ຮູ້ວ່າESL ແມ່ນໝາຍເຖິງຫຍັງ? ຕອນຂ້ອຍມາຮຽນເທື່ອທຳອິດຂ້ອຍຄິດວ່າ ESL ໝາຍເຖິງ E=ແມ່ນພາສາອັງກິດ(English). S=ແມ່ນພາສາທີສອງ(second). L=ແມ່ນ ພາສາ(language).

ຫຼັງຈາກທີ່ຂ້ອຍໄດ້ເຂົ້າມາຮຽນຢູ່ທີ່ນີ້ຂ້ອຍໄດ້ຮູ້ວິທີ່ຮຽນພາສາອັງກິດທີ່ຖຶກຕ້ອງຕາມຫຼັກ ໄວຍາກອນຂອງພາສາອັງກິດຂ້ອຍໄດ້ຮຽນເວົ້າພາສາອັງກິດໃຫ້ຖຶກຕາຫຼັກໄວຍາກອນແລະຂ້ອຍກໍ່ ຍັງໄດ້ຮຽນເວົ້າພາສາອັງກິດໃຫ້ຖຶກສຽງແລະອອກສຽງຕາມສຳນຽງ ແລະຂ້ອຍກໍ່ໄດ້ຮູ້ວ່າຄົນທີ່ມາ ຮຽນຢູ່ ESL ນີ້ແມ່ນມາຈາກຫຼາຍບ່ອນຫຼາຍປະເທດແລະຫຼາຍສາດສະໜາທີ່ເຂົ້າມາຮຽນຢູ່ທີ່ນີ້. ຂ້ອຍເອງແມ່ນມາຈາກປະເທດລາວ. ປະຊາຊົນປະໂຕປະຊາຊົນລາວ. ແມ່ນປະເທດທີ່ອ້ອມຮອບດ້ວຍ ແຜ່ນດິນຢູ່ທາງພາກໃຕ້ຂອງທະວີບອາຊິ.ຄົນທີ່ຮຽນຢູ່ຫ້ອງບາງຄົນກໍ່ມາຈາກປະເທດຈີນ ບາງຄົນ ກໍ່ມາຈາກທະວີບເອີຣົບ ບາງຄົນກໍ່ມາຈາກທະວີບອາຟຣິກາ ແລະກໍຍັງມີອີກຫຼາຍປະເທດທີ່ ມ່ຮຽນຢູ່ທີ່ນີ້

ຫຼັງຈາກທີ່ຂ້ອຍໄດ້ເຂົ້າມາຮຽນຢູ່ທີ່ນີ້ຂ້ອຍໄດ້ຮຽນຮູ້ຫຼາຍສິ່ງຫຼາຍຢ່າງບໍ່ແມ່ນວ່າຂ້ອຍນີ້ໄດ້ຮຽນແຕ່ ພາສາອັງກິດຢ່າງດຽວຂ້ອຍກໍ່ໄດ້ຮຽນຮູ້ຫຼາຍສິ່ງຫຼາຍແນວ ແລ້ວຂ້ອຍເອງກໍ່ຍັງໄດ້ຮຽນຮູ້ເລື່ອງ ການດຳລົງຊິວິດຢູ່ປະເທດອາເມລິກາ ແລະກໍ່ຍັງໄດ້ຮຽນຮູ້ການສິ່ສານກັບຄົນຫຼາຍໆປະ ເທດຫຼາຍໆບ່ອນໃນໂລກນີ້ອີກດ້ວຍ

ແລະຂ້ອຍກໍ່ດີໃຈຫຼາຍທີ່ໄດ້ມາຮຽນທີ່ນີ້ທີ່ ESL. ຕອນນີ້ຂ້ອຍສາມາດເວົ້າອັງກິດໄດ້ກໍ່າຂຶ້ນຫຼາຍ ແລະຂ້ອຍກໍ່ມີຄວາມໝັ້ນໃຈໃນໂຕເອງທີ່ຈະກ້າເວົ້າພາສາອັງກິດ

Sticky Rice with Mango

Ingredients:

* 2 cups of cooked sticky rice.
* 1 ½ cup coconut cream.
* ½ tsp of salt.
* 2 ripe sweet mangoes.

1. Heat coconut cream in a sauce pan with salt until hot (not boiling), and add sugar and stir until all is dissolved.
2. Add the cooked sticky rice and stir frequently so it doesn't stick to the pan, and let simmer 5 minutes.
3. Turn off stove and cook for 30 minutes, then rice will continue to absorb the cream.
4. Serve with sliced mangoes: sprinkle toasted sesame seeds for added crunch

Amphonnaly Thamavongsa
laos

ເຂົ້າໜຽວໝາກມ່ວງ

+ ສ່ວນປະກອບ

* 2 ຖ້ວຍເຂົ້າໜຽວທີ່ສຸກແລ້ວ

* 1½ ຖ້ວຍນ້ອຍ. ນ້ຳກະທິໝາກພ້າວ

* ½ ບ່ວງກາເຟ. ເກືອ

* ½ ຖ້ວຍນ້ອຍ. ນ້ຳຕານ

* 2 ໜ່ວຍໝາກມ່ວງ

1. ເອົາກະທິໝາກພ້າວໃສ່ໝໍ້ ເອົາເກືອໃສ່ເອົານ້ຳຕານໃສ່ ແລ້ວຕົ້ມໃຫ້ນ້ຳກະທິຮ້ອນ (ໂດຍບໍ່ມັນຜິດແຮງ) ເບິ່ງວ່ານ້ຳຕານແລະກະທິເຂົ້າກັນແລ້ວ

2. ເອົາເຂົ້າໜຽວທີ່ກວນໄວ້ໃສ່ ຫຼຸງຈາກຄົນໃຫ້ເຂົ້າກັນປະມານ 5ນາທີ

3. ຫຼຸງຈາກນັ້ນມອດເຕົາໄຟແລະປະໃຫ້ມັນເຢັນປະມານ 30ນາທີ ຖ້າໃຫ້ເຂົ້າເຢັນ

4. ແລ້ວກໍເອົາມາກິນກັບໝາກມ່ວງ ຫຼືເອົາໝາກກ້ວຍມາໃສ່ເພື່ອໃຫ້ມັນຫວານ

At first, I was nervous about learning English in the ESL class, but I made some progress as the time went by.

We did many presentations with news in the ESL class. Questions were made based on the news. Our teacher helped us to write complete sentences with these questions and she corrected them when it was necessary.

Also, we learned grammar from her. Grammar is the basic way to make correct sentences. Knowing the parts of speech helped us place them in the right order in sentences.

Although I had taken this class two years ago, I learned more and it becomes clear to me now. As I prepared for the test, I looked up more words and I learned to spell them correctly. By spelling correctly, I have memorized more words.

I am still having difficult with speaking, reading and writing, but I have a better understanding of English grammar now than when I took the ESL class the first time.

Lastly, I learned good study habits. For example, let's say we came late to class or we did not raise our hands when our teacher asked questions, we did not do our homework or when we did not speak English in class with people next to us, we had to give away one ESL dollar. On the other hand, when we raised our hands to answer questions and participated, we received ESL dollars. On the last day of class we are able to buy school supplies and other merchandise.

Now, I am not afraid of meeting a Native American in the street. I have the courage to speak to them. I have a hope about the future when I will be able to relax when I speak. The day will come when I will make friends with them and will participate in American society.

Ok Sun Hong
Korea

ESL를 통해서

처음엔 이에스엘 글래스가 긴장이 되었지만 영어를 배우면서 많은 발전하게 되었습니다.

클래스애서 매주 뉴스를 준비해서 발표를 합니다.여기에 우리는 질문을 만듭니다. 라모스 선생님은 이 질문과 대답이 완전희 맞을때까지 고쳐 주십니다.

또한 문법을 배웠습니다. 문법은 문장을 만드는데 기본 구조 입니다. 문장의 8가지구조를 통해문장을 만드는 구조와 위치를 배웠습니다.

2년 전에도 배웠지만 이번 태스트를 통해 얼마나 발전 했는지를 알게 되었습니다.

단어 태스트를하는데 이것을 통해 단어를 보다 정확이 알게 되었고 단어도 더많이 외우게 되었습니다.

아직도 말하고 읽고 쓰고 듣는것을 잘 못하지만 지금은 이 전보다 문법과 이해력이 많이 높아졌습니다.

마지막으로 공부하는 좋은 습관을 배웠습니다. 예를들면, 수업을 늦게 오거나, 선생님의 질문에 손을 들지 않고 대답을 하거나, 숙제를 안해 오거나, 다른 친구에게 영어로 말하지 않을 때에는 벌로 선생님이 만든 1 달러를 빼았깁니다. 그러나 숙제를 잘하거나 선생님의 질문에 손을 들고 대답을 맞으면 1달를 받게 됩니다. 우리는 달러를 모두모아서 마지막 날에 학용품을 살수 있습니다.

지금 나는 거리에서 미국 사람을 만나도 두려워하지 않습니다.그만큼 말하는데 용기가 생겼습니다. 나는 앞으로 영어로 말하는데 좀더 편안하게 대화 하길 원하고 그리고 더욱 미국 사회에 친밀하게 될것입니다.

Ok Sun Hong
Korea

Hot and Spicy Rice cake

Ingredients :

    300 grams of tubes rice cake
    4 tsp hot pepper paste
    1 Tsp sugar
    4 cups of water
    8 large dried anchovies
    3 green onions
    2 fish cakes

Directions:

1. Separate the tubes of rice cake into individual pieces.
2. Pour 4 cups of water and add 8 large dried, cleaned anchovies. Boil the water for 10 minutes over medium heat.
3. Remove the anchovies and add the rice cakes, 4Tsp of hot pepper paste, 1 Tsp of sugar, 2 fish cakes and 1 Tsp of hot pepper flakes. Stir it constantly.
4. Cut 3 green onions into 1 inch long pieces, and add them to the pot.
5. Keep stirring until the sauce is thick and the rice cake is shiny.
6. Serves 5

떡복기만들기.

재료:

떡 300 그램

고추장 4 숫가락

설탕 1 숫가락

물 4 컵

마른 멸치 8 개

파 3 개

어묵 2 개

1. 떡들을 분리해놓는다.

2. 푸라이 판에 네컵정도 물을붓고 머리와 내장을 재거한 큰멸치 8 개를
추가한다. 중간불에 10 분정도 끓인다.

3. 멸치를 재하고, 떡을넣고, 네스폰정도의 고추장, 설탕 1 스폰정도를 추가한후 계속 젓는다.

4. 파 3 개를 1cm 크기로 잘라서 끓는 물속에 넣는다.

5. 양념이 걸죽해지고 떡이 부드러울때까지 젓는다.

6.5 명정도에게 대접한다.

   Ok Sun Hong ESL

I love this ESL course. It is a very good environment to learn English and understand what we learn.

In this course there are four parts: listening, speaking, reading and writing. This is a very good method to improve our English.

Every morning we report news, which helps us to improve our reading and speaking. We can find something on the Internet news or newspapers then bring it to the classroom and read it.

I think this is a good way to increase our English vocabulary. I think we can do this just once a week.

Finally, I hope this course can be open forever, because here there is a very good teacher and very good students. Every day there are new things waiting for me.

Liang Piao
Korea

ESL

我很喜欢这个ESL课程，他是一个很好的环境去学习英语很理解所学的内容的地方

在这个课程里，包括四个部分听说读写，这是一个可以很有效的方法去提高学习的数度，每

天早上我们都会有度新闻的环节，他可一帮助提高我们的读和说。我有一个很好的想法，我们可

以多家一个内容，就是自己在网上找一些内容，之后在背诵下来，在课堂上呢背下你所记住的东

西，这样科技增加英语的词汇量，但这只是我个人的一个想法，可以一个星期一次，和新闻一样

最后，希望这个课程可以永远的开下去，因为这里有很好的老师和很好的学生，每天都有新

奇的事情等着我们.

Liang Piao
China

Ingredients

材料：
1：一磅韭菜
2：四个鸡蛋
3：一茶匙盐
4：十茶匙油

做法：

1：在碗里把鸡蛋打碎，把韭菜

切成一厘米的段。

2：用锅加热油后，倒入鸡蛋在油中，

当鸡蛋凝固后，移除锅中。

3： 把韭菜放入锅中，一分钟后把鸡蛋
也放回锅中，一起炒，加盐。

4：当试尝口感很好时，移除他们到盘子里
好了，可以吃了，这些足够一对夫妻吃

Liang Piao
China

Scrambled Eggs with Leek

Ingredients

1lb leek
4 eggs
I tsp. salt
10 tsp. Oil

Directions:

1. Crack the eggs in a bowl
2. Cut leeks into one inch pieces
3. Heat oil in pan and add eggs
4. Remove eggs from pan when formed
5. Put the leeks into the pan for about one minute; put the eggs back in the pan and scramble them with salt
6. Transfer to a plate
7. Serves about two people

Liang Piao
China

I feel that in class room I'm learning more every day on different subjects.

I can start to read and understand what I need to do. I'm starting to be able to pick out my news form the newspaper and read some of the articles printed in the newspaper. I feel I have picked up a lot of the news that is covered everyday in school.

I have started to understand the difference between singular and plural. That helps me to understand more of the English Language.

Pyong Cloutier
Korea

나는 교실에서 매일 많은 것을 배우고 있음을 느낍니다.

나는 나는 내가 필요한 것을 이해하고, 읽는 것을 시작할 수 있습니다. 나는 신문에서 뉴스를 골라서 기사를 읽을 수 있게 되었습니다. 학교 수업을 위해 매일 많은 뉴스를 읽었습니다.

나는 단수와 복수의 차이점을 이해하기 시작했습니다.

이것들은 내가 영어를 이해하는데 많이 도움이 되었습니다.

Pyong Cloutier
Korea

Rice soup

Ingredients

1 cup rice cakes (sliced)
3 cups water
2 cloves garlic
1 tsp beef stock
1/2 tsp salt and pepper
1 egg
1 tsp ground beef

Directions

1. Put water and beef stock into a pot.
2. Put sliced rice cake, minced garlic into the pot of boiling water.
3. Cook for 10-15 minutes until tender.
4. Fry egg, add ground beef.
5. Put the rice soup into a bowl.
6. Put egg and ground beef in dish and add salt and pepper.

Pyong Cloutier
Korea

떡국

‹재료›

떡국떡 1컵
물 3컵
마늘 2쪽
소고기 다시다 1술
소금, 후추 1작은술
계란 1개
다진 소고기 1큰술

‹조리법›

1. 물과 다시다를 냄비에 넣는다.
2. 물이 끓으면 떡국떡과 다진 마늘을 넣는다.
3. 떡이 익을 때까지 10-15분정도 끓인다.
4. 계란은 지단을 만들어 썰고 다진 소고기는 볶는다.
5. 떡이 익으면 그릇에 담는다.
6. 계란과 소고기를 얹고 기호에 따라 소금과 후추를 뿌린다.

Pyong Cloutier
Korea

I moved to the United States six years ago. Upon my arrival I found myself frustrated and insecure due to my inability to communicate. Coming from a place where my job as a journalist required constant exposure to people and free expression of ideas and then all of a sudden not being able to say what I was thinking was quite frustrating.

I therefore decided to enroll at the ESL program at CTC with the Adult Education department in order to overcome this limitation; and since then my life has completely changed. I was able to complete the program in a year, become a United Citizen, and now I hold a supervisory position.

The impact of ESL on my life is something that I can see on a daily basis, at work, at home, in social activities. My life is so much easier and joyful because I can express my ideas with some confidence.

I have made new friends, am able to travel without any difficulties, and most importantly I am able to communicate my ideas to others. I no longer feel insecure. On the contrary, I feel empowered.

Thanks to ESL I'm getting better every day and everything is easier in my life. These programs help a lot of people like me and I will recommend this program because they really work.

Roxidania Karron
Honduras

Me traslade a los Estados Unidos hace seis años. A mi llegada me encontré frustrada he insegura hacia mi falta de habilidad para comunicarme. De un lugar donde mi trabajo como periodista requiere la constante exposición a las personas y la libre expresión de mis ideas y de repente no puede decir lo que pensaba era frustrante.

Por lo tanto, decidí inscribirme en el programa para adultos de ESL a fin de superar esta limitación, y desde entonces mi vida ha cambiado por completo. He tenido la oportunidad de completar el programa y mi estatus en un año, a ser un ciudadano de los Estados, y ahora mantengo una posición de supervisora.

El impacto de ESL en mi vida es algo que puedo ver a diario en el trabajo, en casa y en las actividades sociales, mi vida es mucho más fácil y feliz porque puedo expresar mis ideas con confianza.

He hecho nuevos amigos, soy capaz de viajar sin ninguna dificultad, y lo más importante es que soy capaz de comunicar mis ideas a los demás. Ya no me siento insegura por el contrario me siento empoderada.

Gracias al programa de ESL estoy mejorando cada día y todo es más fácil en mi vida, estos programas ayudan a muchas personas como yo con deseos de superación, en lo particular yo recomiendo estos programas, ya que realmente si funcionan.

Chicken in coconut milk

Ingredients

1 whole medium chicken.
1 small can of coconut milk.
1 quarter cup of coconut cream.
1 medium onion chopped.
1 tbsp chopped garlic
1 tbsp black pepper.
Salt to taste.
2 tbsp chopped cilantro
A pinch of sugar

Preparation

1. Remove skin from the chicken and wash
2. Season with all the ingredients
3. Fry for 10 minutes
4. Gradually add coconut milk and coconut cream
5. Simmer for 30 minutes

Roxidania Karron
Honduras

Pollo en leche de coco.

Ingredientes

1. pollo entero mediano
1. lata pequeña de leche de coco.
1. cuarto de taza de crema de coco.
1. cebolla mediana picada.
1. cucharada sopera de ajo picado
1. cucharada sopera de pimienta negra. Sal al gusto.
2. cucharada de cilantro picado
Una pizca de azúcar

Preparacion

1. Lave el pollo con agua y retire la piel.
2. luego agrege los condimentos mencionados antes
3. sorfreir durante 10 minutos,
4. añadir poco a poco la leche de coco y la crema de coco
5. cocine a fuego lento durante 30 minutos.

During the ESL program, I have had the opportunity to meet international spouses from different countries such as Korea, The Philippines, Venezuela, Puerto Rico, Honduras, Nicaragua, Samoa, etc.

All of us are living a military life style. We go through the same situations when our spouses get deployed. And when they are gone, that is when we realize the importance of knowing English. There are no more husbands/wives advising you or telling you what to do and it is hard when we do not know how to communicate.

For many of us English is difficult because it is not our native language but that's why we are here, to learn English. The ESL program is a great opportunity to learn and improve our English. Maybe it is hard but we need to keep practicing and do not quit. DO NOT GIVE UP!!

One day we will feel very proud of ourselves for everything we have done to survive in this country. We will feel free to go to the bank or the store or anywhere and BE SECURE in the knowledge that we can communicate fluently.

Rubi Hostetter
Mexico

Durante el programa de ESL (Inglés como segunda lengua) he tenido la oportunidad de conocer a esposas/esposos de diferentes países como Corea, Las Filipinas, Venezuela, PuertoRico, Honduras, Nicaragua, Samoa, etc.

Todos nosotros estamos viviendo un estilo de vida militar. Pasamos por las mismas situaciones cuando nuestros esposas/esposos tienen misiones en el exterior. Y cuando ellos se van es cuando nos damos cuenta de la importancia de saberInglés. Ya no hay más esposos/esposas aconsejándote o diciéndote que hacer y eso es difícil cuando nosotros no sabemos cómo comunicarnos.

Para muchos de nosotros el inglés es difícil porque no es nuestro idioma nativo pero es por eso que estamos aquí, para aprender Inglés. El programa de ESL es una gran oportunidad para aprender y mejorar nuestro Inglés. Tal vez es difícil pero tenemos que seguir practicando y no renunciar. Nunca te des por vencido!!

Un día nos sentiremos orgullosos de nosotros mismos por todo lo que hemos hecho para sobrevivir en este país. Nos sentiremos libres de ir al banco o a la tienda o a cualquier lugar y estar seguros de que podemos comunicarnos con fluidez.

Rubi Hostetter
Mexico

Ingredients:

- 4 large eggs
- 1 tablespoon water
- 1 tablespoon salsa (your favorite, but it should be chunky)
- 1 tablespoon butter
- 1 tablespoon olive oil
- 4 corn tortillas, torn into small pieces
- 1/4 cup finely chopped white onion
- 2 teaspoons minced fresh cilantro
- 2/3 cup grated Monterrey jack cheese

Directions:

1-lightly beat the eggs, water and salsa together in a small bowl and set aside.
2-Warm the butter and olive oil in a heavy skillet.
3-Add the tortilla pieces and sauté until softened. Add the chopped onion and sauté until it is transparent.
4-Pour the egg mixture into the skillet, and scramble until the eggs are done.
5-Remove the skillet from the heat, and sprinkle the cilantro and cheese into the eggs, again stirring well.

Rubi Hostetter
Mexico

Migas Mexicanas

Ingredientes:

- 4 huevos grandes
- 1 cucharada de agua
- 1 cucharada de salsa (su favorita, pero debe ser gruesa)
- 1 cucharada de mantequilla
- 1 cucharada de aceite de oliva
- 4 tortillas de maíz, cortadas en trozos pequeños
- 1/4 taza de cebolla blanca finamente picada
- 2 cucharadas de cilantro fresco
- 2/3 taza de queso Monterrey Jack

Instrucciones:

1- En un tazón pequeño, bate ligeramente los huevos, el agua y la salsa, y déjalos a un lado reposar.
2- Calienta la mantequilla y el aceite de oliva en un sartén.
3- Añade los trozos de tortilla hasta que se ablanden. Añade la cebolla picada y fríela hasta que esté transparente.
4- Vierte la mezcla de los huevos en el sartén yrevuelve hasta que el huevo se haya cocido bien.
5. Retira el sartén del fuego y espolvorea el cilantro y el queso en los huevos y agítalos bien.

Rice and Fish

Ingredients:

Vegetable oil
Fish (3)
Rice
Parsley
Tomato paste
3 carrots
1 eggplant
1 cassava root
½ of Cauliflower
Smoked fish
2 onions and 2 cloves of garlic chopped in small pieces
Green pepper
Red and dark pepper
1 cube magi

INSTRUCTIONS

1. Mix the Chile, pepper, garlic, parsley and a bit of onions in a blender; make a small cut on the fish and fill with the mixture.
2. Heat the oil; add a little bit of chopped onion and garlic in the oil and cook until golden brown, then remove them from the oil.
3. Fry the fish on both sides for about 5 min; remove the fish from the oil and keep them on a plate.
4. Reduce the heat and add the tomato paste in the oil and stir for about 5 min.
5. Add water and the vegetables; cook for about 50 min; add the fish (include the smoked fish). Reduce the heat and wait another 30 min.
6. Remove the veggies and fish and keep them in a bowl.

7. Blend the red and black pepper, garlic, onion, green pepper, magi and salt and add in the sauce.
8. Wash the rice and put in the microwave for 5 min; remove it from the microwave, stir the rice and put it back in the microwave for another 5 min; remove the rice from the microwave.
9. Add the precooked rice to the sauce, mix and cover the pot; stir from time to time.
10. Wait until the rice is cooked to serve.

Note: you have to clean the fish and peel the cassava root and carrots.
When you put the rice in the microwave, make sure that all the water is drained from the rice.

Thieboudienne

Huile d'arachide
Riz
3 poissons persey tomate concentre huile d'arachide
3 carrotes,
1 aubergine
Du manioc
½ chou-fleur poisson sale
2 onions et ailes coupes en petit morceaux
Poivron vert
Piment et poivre
1 cube maggi

Instruction

1. Pilez le piment, poivre, persy, ailes et un peu d'oignon dans un mortier. Faire un petit trou sur chaque poisson et y inserrez le mélange.
2. Chauffez l'huile dans une marmite, ajoutez un peu d'oignon et d'aile decoupes en petits morceaux dans l'huile chaud .
3. Frire les poissons pour une duree de 5 mn, puis les retirer.(Frire les deux cotes).
4. Reduire le feu, ajoutez le tomate concentre dans l'huile et le remuez constament pour une duree de 5mn.
5. Ajoutez l'eau et les legumes. Laissez les cuire pour une duree de 50mn, puis ajoutez les poissons sans oublier le poisson sale.
6. Attendre 30 mn pour retirer les poissons et les legumes. Gardez les a chaud dans un bol ferme.
7. Pilez l'oignon, le piment, poivre, ailes, poivron vert, maggi et sel dans un mortier et ajoutez le mélange dans la marmite.

8. Lavez le riz et le precuisiner au microonde pour 5mn. Sortir le bol du riz, remuez le riz et le remettre dans le microonde pour une autre duree de 5mn.
9. Ajoutez le riz sur la sauce du marmite, melangez le tout puis fermez la marmite. Remuez le riz de temps en temps.
10. Servir au cuisson.

It's an immense pleasure for me to participate in this activity. I took English as a Second Language with the best English teacher ever during the Spring-Fall of 2009. My experience was very great. Taking an ESL class really shaped my knowledge of academic English. When I first came to the United-States I could not communicate at all with other people or understand them. I was too shy to talk in a foreign language and I also used to pronounce the English words very badly. Then I took this class. There, I learned a lot. My classmates and I studied a lot of grammar such as the use of correct punctuation, articles, prepositions . . . We also learned how to use the English tense by doing a lot of conjugations such as the present tense, present progressive, past perfect. look at the key word as a guide . . . Reading was very important because it helped me articulate the English worlds correctly, get rid of my accent a little and at the same time, my vocabulary was getting richer. After each lecture, we used to write some sentences about each new word we learned. My favorite part was the news. The students were supposed to write and bring news articles and read them in front of the class. We got a lot of important information that helped us understand what was going on around the world and debate it. Without forgetting the field trips, I am still saving my coins that I received from the mayor of Killeen. Anyway, It was really a great experience. My classmates used to be a second family for me. I miss them all Seoyoung, Zhenya, Kim . . . my instructor who is so nice and supportive even though I had been there for like seven months. She will call or send an email to check on me, ask how I am doing with my classes. She really wants her students to succeed. I am just very lucky to have had her as my instructor because, not only could I write and express myself, but I was also able to enroll in college courses in order to realize my career aspiration.

Sokhna Daga Fall
Senegal, Africa

Salut tout le monde. C'est avec un grand plaisir que j'ai decide de participer a ce projet. J'avais pris l' anglais comme une seconde language avec la meilleure ESL instutitrice durant le printemps a l'automne deux mille neuf. Mon experience etait riche. Quand je venais juste des Etats-Unis, je ne pouvasi ni communiquer encore moins comprendre ce que les autres disaient. J'etais tres timide de communiquer avec une langue etrangere que je ne maitriser pas. C'est alors que j'avais pris la decision d'approfondir ma connaissance sur la langue anglaise. Mes camarade de classe et moi avions appris beaucoup de choses comme a conjuguer les temps au present, passe, futur et present progressive. Nous avions aussi fait beacoup de grammaire, tel que l'utilisation du ponctuation, de l'article, preposition en anglais. La lecture etait aussi importante parce que ca nous permettrait de prononcer les mots corrrectement, d'eleminer notre accent et en meme temps, notre vocabulaire devenait de plus en plus riche. Pour chaque lecture, y'avait de nouveaux mots a apprendre et pour chaque nouveau mot appris, l'eleve devrait ecrire une sentence.

Mon activite prefere etait l'information hebdomadaire. Chaque matin, on devrait amener une information que nous devrions partager avec le reste de la classe. Cela nous permettrait d'etre informer et de comprendre ce qui se passé aux Etats-Unis et le reste du monde. Il y'avait aussi les petites sorties que l'institutrice organisait. Un des plus symboliques etait notre visite chez le maire de Killeen Timothy Hancock avec qui j'ai eu l'occasion de questioner sur l'immigration.

Mes camarades de classe etaient une seconde famille pour moi. Elles me manquent tous, Seoyoung, Zhenya et Kim. Elles etaient vraiment tres gentilles et supportives. Bien que je n'ai passé que sept mois la-bas, mon institutrice m'appelle ou m'envoie de l'email pour s'acquerir de mes nouvelles et voire comment je progresse avec mes classes. Elle veut vraiment que ses eleves reussissent. Je suis tres fortune de l'avoir comme institutrice parce que après un certains moment, je pouvais ecrire et m'exprimer en anglais. Je suis plus confiante a moi meme et maintenant je suis au college pour devenir operationelle.

Sokhna daga Fall
Senegal, Africa

½ cup of oil
Riz
3 poissons
persey
2 onions, coupes en petit morceaux
1 poivron vert
2 pots de tomate concentre
huile d'arachide
3 carrotes,
1 aubergine
du manioc
1 cube maggi
2 Oignon, ailes
Piment et poivre

Instruction

1. piler le persy, piment, poivre, ailes et ¼ de l'oignon dans un mortier. Faire un petit trou sur chaque poisson et y inserrer le mélange.
2. Chauffer l'huile dans un marmite, ajouter un autre ¼ d'oignon et de l'aile decoupes en petits morceaux dans l'huile chaud suivie des poissons pour une duree de 10 mn puis les retirer.
3. Reduire le feu et ajouter le tomate concentre dans l'huile et au bout de 5mn, ajouter de l'eau et les legumes, laisser mijoter pour une duree de 30mn, puis ajouter les poissons. Attendre une autre 30 mn pour retirer les poissons et les legumes, garder les a chaud dans un bol avec couverture.
4. Ajouter dans la sauce le mélange de l'oignon, piment, poivre, aile, poivron vert, cube maggi et sel deja piles dans le mortier
5. Ajouter le riz, ensuite melanger le tout, remuer de temps en temps. Servir au cuisson.

Wolof

diweline
Tiebe
3 djeunes
roffe
Tomate lokati
3 carottes
1 Bassanete
½ soupame
1 Gnambi
guedji
Soble ak ladj
Cani salade vert
Cani ak pobare
1 cube maggi

1. Debale rof, cani, pobare ak touti sobele. Defale reude si djeune bi, dade si dougale rof bi.
2. Tangalale diweline bamou tangue, dougalale touti sobele ak ladje bi nga dagate pare, haral bamou doree.
3. Safale djeune yi apres nga seppi lene.
4. Wagnile tale bi, def si tomate bi, nga yeugueule ko ba 5mn, ngaye soguadi gnoulogue.
5. Dougalale legumes yi si gnoulouke bi, legui nga hare 50mn bala nga si dougale djeune bi. So yoke djeune bi, wagnile gas bi, dadi barale pour 30mn.
6. Sepile djeune yi ak legumes yi, ci bol bou ame coubere après nga teudje lene.
7. Defare sa nokoss, dadi debou sobele, cani salade ak cani, pobare, ladje, horome, cube maggi da dilene dougale si tiine bi.
8. Rahassale tiebe bi après nga taye.
9. Legui nga dougale tiebe bi, dadi diakhasse lep bamou masse. Deko eulbeti si digane tebi.
10. Togale hare ba tiebe gnore nga yake.

I had not studied English before I joined the U.S military. One day I heard about this ESL school on post and I joined the class and started to study English.

At first, I had trouble combining study with work, but I was able to gradually adapt. I started to find my own studying method while I attended class and listened to the teacher and other students talking. I wasted a lot of time when I didn't find a way to study to fit me, but gradually I came across my own way of studying.

I practiced reading and speaking, and I was able to improve my listening while I listened to the teacher and other students' conversation. I memorized a word every day, I learned the way how to write longer sentences, and I tried reading and understanding newspapers by doing homework. I tried to improve so other people would understand my English.

I still can't speak perfect English though. The ESL class has influenced me to keep studying English after the class was over.

I learned this from ESL class. I think the ESL class was a very valuable opportunity for me, because now I have more confidence to work. I'm not scared any more, and I have a good habit to focus more carefully when people are talking.

Kyoung Kim
Korea

저는 미군에 입대하기 전까지 영어를 공부해 본 적이 없었습니다. 어느 날 부대 내에 있는 ESL 수업에 대해 듣게 되었고 수업에 참여하여 공부를 시작하게 되었습니다.

처음에는 일과 공부를 병행하는데 어려움이 있었지만 점점 적응을 할 수 있었습니다.수업에 참석하여 선생님과 다른 학생들이 말하는 것을 들으면서 저는 저만의 공부 방법을 찾기 시작했습니다.나에게 맞는 공부 방법을 찾기 전에는 많은 시간을 허비했지만 점차 나만이 공부방법을 찾게 되었습니다.

저는 읽기와 말하기를 연습하였고 선생님과 다른 학생들이 이야기하는 것을 들으며 듣기능력을 향상시킬 수 있었습니다. 숙제를 하면서 매일 단어 하나씩을 외웠고, 긴 문장을 쓰는 법을 배웠고, 신문을 읽고 이해하려고 노력하였습니다. 그리고 다른 사람들이 제가 하는 영어를 더 잘 이해할 수 있도록 노력하였습니다.

아직 영어를 완벽하게 말할 수는 없지만 이 ESL 수업은 수업과정이 끝난 후에도 제가 영어 공부를 계속할 수 있게 하는 동기가 되어 주었습니다.

저는 ESL 수업을 통해 이것을 배웠습니다.저는 군대에서 일을 할 때 더 이상 두려워하지 않으며, 이전보다 훨씬 더 자신감을 갖고 일을 하게 되었고, 또 사람들이 말할 때 더 주의 깊게 집중하는 좋은 습관을 가질 수 있게 되었기 때문에 이 ESL 수업은 저에게 매우 귀중한 기회였다고 생각합니다.

Kim-Bap

(Ingredients)

10 sheets—Seaweed
10 pieces—Pickled Radish
10 pieces—Ham
10 pieces—Boiled fish paste
10 pieces—Burdock
10 pieces—Cucumber
5 cups—White rice
2 cups—Sesame oil
½ cups—Sea salt
¼ cups—sesame seeds

(Directions)

1. Cook rice
2. Add sesame oil, sea salt, sesame seeds.
3. Mix rice and other ingredients together.
4. Prepare Seaweed with rice and put ingredients.
5. Make a roll.
6. Cut the roll in pieces.

Spc. Kyoung Kim
Korea

김 밥

(재료)

김 10장
절인 무 10개
햄 10개
오뎅 10개
우엉 10개
오이 10개
백미 5컵
참기름 2컵
소금 1/2컵
깨소금 1/4컵

(조리법)

1. 밥을 짓는다.
2. 참기름, 소금, 깨소금을 넣는다.
3. 밥과 다른 재료들을 함께 섞는다.
4. 김 위에 밥을 놓고 다른 재료들을 올린다.
5. 둘둘 만다.
6. 조각 내어 썬다.

ESL stands for English as a Second Language. This ESL program has teachers who help students to develop their speaking, writing, reading, and comprehension skills with the English language and help students become more fluent in English.

When I first came to the United Sates I didn't know English. I had difficulty communicating with people, especially when I had a doctor's appointment. I needed to have an interpreter with me all the time. Then I realized that I need to go to school. For someone like me, I can't afford to pay for ESL classes because I don't make enough money. I searched for free classes; I was blessed to find this class for free even though it took me a long time on the waiting list. When they called me to come to class I came with a great deal of enthusiasm and motivation. Believe me, now I am enjoying the ESL class. I appreciate the hard work that I get from our class. I learn how to use correct sentences when I speak. I learned how to use verbs my first day in class. I didn't know the correct grammar, and now I am so impressed.

I like the varying ethnic and cultural backgrounds of everyone in the class. In my opinion, ESL programs help me break down and learn mathematics and History in a way that is easier for me because I have English as a second language. The Students who do not understand English cannot understand or sometimes read instructions. Classes such as US History would be a lot harder to understand if they do not know simple rules of the English language.

I look forward to improving my speaking and understanding of English as it is vital for success in today's international world because the international language is English.

Widad Salim
Sudan

Widad Salim's essay (Arabic)

اللغة الإنجليزية :ـ كلغة ثانية للنطقيين بغيرها ؛ هذا البرنامج لديها المعلمين الذين يساعدون الطلاب على تطوير في تحدث اللغة، والكتابة، والقراءة، ومهارات الفهم في اللغة الإنجليزية ومساعدة الطلاب على أن يصبحوا أكثر طلاقة في اللغة الإنجليزية.

عندما جئت لاول مرة الى الولايات المتحدة لم أكن ان أعرف اللغة الإنجليزية بصورة جيد. كان لي صعوبة في التواصل مع الناس وخصوصا، اذا كانت عند موعد مع الطبيب. كنت بحاجة لمترجم في كل وقت. ثم أدركت أنني بحاجة للذهاب إلى المدرسة. لشخص مثلي، وأنا لا أملك مع ادفعه لتعليم اللغة النجليزية كلغة ثانية لأنني لا احصل ما يكفي من المال. قومت ببحث عن دروس مجانية، وكنت مباركة للعثور على هذه صف المدرسي المجانا على الرغم من استغرق مني وقتا طويلا في قائمة الانتظار. عندما أتصلوا لي أن آتي إلى المدرسة جئت مع قدرا كبيرا من الحماس والدافعية.

صدقوني الآن أنا أتتمتع بالصف كثيرا. وأقدر العمل الشاق من أتجاه المدرسة. لقد أتعلمت كيفية استخدام جمل صحيحة عندما أتكلم. وأتعلمت كيفية استخدام الافعال في أول يوم دخلولي في الصف. لم أكن أن أعرف النحو الصحيح من قبل ، والآن أعجبا بذلك.

وفي هذه الصف أحبيت متفاوتة العرقية والخلفية الثقافية للجميع من مختلفة أنحاء العالم. وفي رأيي، ان هذه البرنامج اللغة الانجليزية كلغة ثانية يساعد على الفهم وتعلم الرياضيات والتاريخ في أسهل الطريقة ممكن. الطلاب الذين لا يفهمون اللغة الإنجليزية لا يمكنهم فهم أو قراءة، الأحيان تعليمات. والطبقات مثل تاريخ الولايات المتحدة ستكون أصعب بكثير لفهم إذا كانوا لا يعرفون قواعد البسيطة للغة الإنجليزية.

مستقبلاً أنا أتطلع إلى تحسين وفهم اللغة الإنجليزية كما أنه أمر حيوي لتحقيق النجاح في عالم اليوم، لان اللغة الإنجليزية هي اللغة الدولي.

من طرف : وداد سالم
جمهورية جنوب السودان ـ أفريقيا

Sudanese Tamia

Ingredients:

500g chickpeas
4 cloves garlic
2 onions
2 tbsp flour
1 white bread roll
1 tsp baking powder
1 tsp black pepper
1 tsp salt
oil
1 tsp coriander seeds (optional)
1 tsp sesame seeds (optional)
bunch of fresh coriander (optional)
1 green pepper (optional)

method of preparation:

1. Soak chickpeas in water for at least 3 hours.
2. Cook until tender and mix with garlic, onion, pepper and fresh coriander.
3. Soak bread in water.
4. Add with flour to mixture.
5. Stir and add salt, pepper, coriander seeds and pet stand for 15-minutes.
6. Add baking powder.
7. Shape with hands into small saucer.
8. Sprinkle with sesame seeds, Deep fry.
Serve alone, or as a tamia sandwich.

Widad Salim
Juba-South Sudan

المكونات: طامية

500 خرام الحمص ، 4 فصوص من الثوم ، 2 بصل ، 2 ملعقة كبيرة دقيق ، 1 لفة الخبز الأبيض ، 1 مسحوق الخبز ملعقة صغيرة ، 1 ملعقة صغيرة من الفلفل الأسود ، 1 ملعقة صغيرة ملح ، زيت

1 ملعقة شاي بذور الكزبرة (اختياري)

1 ملعقة شاي بذور السمسم (اختياري)

حفنة من الكزبرة الطازجة (اختياري)

1 فلفل أخضر (اختياري)

طريقة التحضير:

1.نقع الحمص في الماء لمدة لا تقل عن 3 ساعات.

2. طهي حتى يصبح طريا ومع الكزبرة والثوم والبصل والفلفل والطازجة.

3. نقع الخبز في الماء إضافة إلى خليط الدقيق.

4. يحرك المزيج أضيفي الملح والفلفل.

5. وبذور الكزبرة وتترك لمدة 15 دقيقة.

6. إضافة مسحوق الخبز.

7. وشكل اليدين في شكل الصغيرة.

8. ويرش مع بذور السمسم.

وداد سالم - جوبا جمهورية جنوب السودان

When I arrived in the United States, one of my goals was to learn English. I was informed and I gathered all the paper work needed to enroll in the ESL course. This was and still is a great opportunity to learn the English language and was the first step to accomplish my goal.

My first day in class was kind of strange but exciting at the same time; mainly because the class consisted of students from different parts of the world and listening to all the different languages was a new experience for me.

I enjoyed going to class because my teacher always made the class interesting and we always had fun while learning. That made the three and a half hours of class go very fast and a great learning experience.

My teacher gave us exercises and tasks every day and we interacted in class. It was one of the best ways for me not to be afraid to speak in public. I am grateful and proud to say thanks to my teacher and the ESL program I learned the basics and will continue to learn English.

Yesenia Fuentes
Mexico

Cuando llegue a este pais, una de mis metas fue aprender el idioma ingles. Me informe e inscribi en la clase de ESL, por que se me hizo una gran oportunidad para aprender elidioma y dar el primer paso para lograr mimeta.

Mi primer dia en la clasefue extrano pero muy emocionantepor que habiamos personas de diferentes partes del mundo y escuchar hablar a mis companeros en diferentes lenguas para mi fue algo Nuevo.

Me encantaba ir a diario la clase siempre hacia la clase muy amena, dinamica y muy personalizada hacia cada uno de nosotros y eso hacia que las 3 horas y media de clase pasaran muy rapido. La maestra nos proporcionaba losllibros didacticos y nos ponia ejercisios muy practicos que nos hacia interactuar entre companeros y eso a mi en lo personal me ayudo mucho para perder el miedo a expresarme. Puedo decir que lo que ahora se del idioma ingles es gracias a mi profesora y las clases de ESL

Yesenia Fuentes
Mexico

Authentic Mexican mole

Ingredients

- 3 tbsp. vegetable oil
- 8 chicken thighs (or use chicken pieces like legs)
- 1 onion, chopped
- 1 green bell pepper, seeded and diced
- 1 poblano pepper, seeded and diced
- 3 cloves garlic, chopped
- 2 tbsp. chili powder
- 2 tsp. ground cumin
- 1/2 tsp. ground cinnamon
- 1 can(14 oz.) fire roasted tomatoes, undrained
- 1/4 cup raisins
- 2 chipotle peppers in adobo sauce, chopped (these are sold in small cans in every grocery store in a Mexican area)
- 1 cup chicken broth
- 1 cup dark Mexican beer, or any dark beer would be fine
- 2 tbsp. peanut butter
- 2 tbsp. sugar
- 1 tsp. salt
- 2 squares (1oz. each) unsweetened chocolate (for baking),

Directions

1. Heat oil in a lg. skillet over medium heat. Add chicken and brown on all sides, set aside.
2. In the same skillet, saute onion, bell pepper, poblano pepper and garlic. Cook and stir until veggies are soft and slightly caramelized. Stir in chili powder, cumin and cinnamon and cook 3 minutes longer.

3. Add tomatoes, raisins, chipotle peppers, chicken broth, beer, peanut butter, sugar and salt. Bring to a simmer and cook 20 minutes, stirring often.
4. Pour the sauce into a blender or food processor and add chocolate. Cover and blend until smooth.
5. Transfer the chicken into the dutch oven, or a deep heavy cooking pot, or skillet. Pour sauce over chicken. Cover and simmer for about 45 minutes, or until chicken is cooked through.
6. Serve warm over cooked white rice with warm tortillas. Garnish with a dollop of sour cream and sprinkle with fresh cilantro, if desired.
7. You will have lots of sauce left-over. Drizzle extra sauce over rice and chicken. The sauce can be frozen and served with chicken later on.

Receta de Mole Mexicano

500 gramos de chiles mulatos

750 gramos de chiles pasillas

750 gramos de chiles anchos

Las tres variedades de chiles van desvenados y despepitados

  450 gramos de manteca de cerdo

5 dientes de ajo medianos

2 cebollas medianas rebanadas

4 tortillas duras partidas en cuatro

1 bolillo frito bien dorado

125 gramos de pasitas

250 gramos de almendras

Pepitas de chile al gusto

150 gramos de ajonjolí

½ cucharada de anís

1 cucharadita de clavo en polvo o 5 clavos de olor

25 gramos de canela en trozo

1 cucharadita de pimienta negra en polvo o 6 pimientas enteras

4 tabletas de chocolate de metate

250 gramos de jitomate pelado y picado

Azúcar y sal al gusto

1 guajolote o pavo grande partido en piezas y cocido en un buen caldo hecho con zanahorias, poro, cebolla, una rama de apio, perejil y un diente de ajo.

PREPARACIÓN

1. Los chiles se pasan por 300 gramos de manteca caliente
2. Se colocan en una cazuela con agua muy caliente y se deja que den un hervor para que se suavicen
3. En la misma manteca se acitronan el ajo y la cebolla, se añaden la tortilla, el pan, las pasas, las almendras, las pepitas de chile, la mitad

del ajonjolí, el anís, el clavo, la canela, las pimientas, el chocolate y el jitomate y se fríe todo muy bien

3. Se agregan los chiles escurridos y se fríe unos segundos más: Todo esto se muele en la licuadora con el caldo donde se coció el pavo y se cuela.

4. En una cazuela de barro especial para mole se pone a calentar el resto de la Manteca

5. Se añade la salsa, se deja hervir el mole durante cinco minutos, se sazona con sal y azúcar y, si es necesario, se añade más caldo; debe quedar una salsa espesita

6. Se deja hervir de 25 a 30 minutos más a fuego lento, se añaden los trozos de guajolote y se deja hervir unos minutos más.

I have been in ESL class for about a month.

Before I started a few of my friends recommended my teacher. They told me "she is kind of strict". So I was nervous. But I enjoy her style of teaching.

One of the things I like about the class is all the students must speak English.

Taking this ESL class helps me with my grammar, vocabulary and spelling. Also the homework helps me a lot. Doing the current news report helps me with my reading. It helps my listening too, because when other classmates read their news, I need to listen carefully, so I can make questions and answers. When I make a wrong sentence, my teacher or other classmates will help me.

My teacher is very good about correcting my grammar. Also she makes me try to correct my mistakes by myself, so I can learn more English.

I hope this ESL class improves my English.

Younghee Prather
Korea

ESL 수업 듣은지도 한달정도 되어 갑니다.

이 수업에 참여하기 전에 몇몇 지인들로 부터 라모스 선생님을 추천받았습니다. 그리고 선생님이 업격 하시다는 말을 듣고 은근히 걱정도 했었습니다. 하지만 오히려 선생님의 그런점이 저의 영어 공부하는데 많은 도움이 되고 있습니다.

수업시간에 영어로만 말 해야 하는것도 마음에 듭니다.

ESL 수업을 통해 문법, 어휘력, 맞춤법에 대해서 많은 도움을 받고 있습니다.

또 최근의 뉴스를 읽고 줄거리를 정림함으로써도 읽기능력도 향상 되고 또 수업중에 다른 사람들이 발표하는것도 잘 경청하여야 하기때문에 듣기능력도 향상 되는거 같습니다. 왜냐하면 다른 사람들의 뉴스를 듣고 질문과 답을 만들어야 하기 때문입니다. 그리고 문법이 틀렸어도 선생님과 다른 사람들이 틀린부분을 바르게 고칠수 있도록 도와 주기 때문입니다.

그리고 선생님께서 항상 저의 잘못된 문법을 올바르게 고쳐 주시고 또한 틀린부분은 저 스스로 고칠수 있도록 해주시기 때문에 저의 더 많이 배울 수 있습니다.

앞으로도 이 ESL 수업을 통해 저의 영어능력이 많은 발전하기를 바랍니다.

Younghee Prather
Korea

Ingredients

1 radish
1 bundle green onion
1/2 cup red pepper powder
1 tablespoon sweet rice powder
1 cup water
1/4 cup apple sauce
1+1/2 tablespoon crushed garlic
1/2 teaspoon crushed ginger root
1+1/2 tablespoon fish sauce
1 tablespoon salted shrimp

Method

1. Cut the radish into 3/4 inch cubes.
2. Put the cubed radish into a bowl and sprinkle salt on radish. Mix and let soak for an hour and rinse.
3. Put 1 tbsp sweet rice powder and 1 cup water into a small pot. Stir until the powder dissolves. Move pot on stove and cook with low heat. Keep stirring until thick, let it cool.
4. Cut the green onion into 1/2 inch pieces.
5. Mix 1/2 cup red pepper powder, sweet rice water, 1+1/2 tbsp smashed garlic, 1/2 tsp smashed ginger root, 1/4 cup apple sauce, 1+1/2 tbsp fish sauce, 1 tbsp salted shrimp.
6. Add the radish, onion and seasoning into a bowl and store in a jar for 24 hours then refrigerate.

Younghee Prather
Korea

깍 두 기

재료

무 1개, 파 1단, 소금 1/2컵, 찹쌀가루 1큰술, 물 1컵, 고춧가루 1/2컵
다진마늘 1+1/2큰술, 다진생강 1/2작은술, 사과 간것 1/4컵
멸치액젓 1+1/2큰술, 새우젓 1큰술

만드는 방법

1. 무를 3/4 인치크기로 썰어준다.
2. 자른 무를 큰 볼에 넣어 준비된 양의 소금은 뿌려 같이 섞어 1시간 동안 담가 두었다가 씻어 준다.
3. 작은 냄비에 찹쌀가루 1큰술과 물 1컵을 넣어 가루가 놓을때까지 저어준다. 가루가 다 눅으면 낮은 불에서 저어가면서 찹쌀풀을 만든다. 찹쌀풀이 다 되었으면 불에서 내려 찹쌀풀을 차갑게 식혀둔다.
4. 준비된 파 1단을 1/2인치 크기로 썰어준다.
5. 큰 불에 고추가루 1/2컵, 찹쌀풀, 다진마늘 1+1/2큰술, 다진생강 1 작은술, 멸치액젓 1+1/2큰술, 새우젓 1큰술, 사과간것 1/4컵을 넣어 같이 섞어준다.
6. 소금에 저리 무와 채썬 파를 위에 5번에 준비한 양념과 함께 버무린다.
7. 용기에 담아 24시간 정도 상온에 둔다.
8. 24시간 상온에서 둔 깍두기를 냉장고에 보관한다. 3-4주 동안 반찬으로 먹으면 된다.

Younghee Prather
Korea

On July 29, I got a text from my husband.

The text was, "You can go to ESL class tomorrow".

I had been waiting for eight months.

On the first day of class, I was excited and afraid. I couldn't concentrate because I was too nervous.

My teacher always wants us to raise our hands when we want to talk.

But that was really hard for me, because I thought "what if I say something incorrectly?, what if I'm wrong?, what if she thinks my questions are weird?" also "what if my classmates sneer at me?" All these thoughts made me afraid.

After one week. She told us something. It was very touching and gave me motivation. She said "if you are wrong, it's ok. Don't be afraid to ask. If someone corrects you? Say thank you. This is how you learn English"

Also, she doesn't say "NO" instead, she says "Somebody else?" or "nice try".

This challenged me to think when I gave a wrong answer.

I think when I was a teenager, I didn't always ask questions and wasn't always interested. I was a normal student. But here in this class, I always try to find the answer, ask lots of questions and study at home.

This is something I learned from this class.

My teacher gives me a motive to learn and challenges me.

Failure is not the end; it will take me to success. I will keep trying and I won't forget this class. I really appreciate my teacher "Ms. Google."

Jin Ha Verheyen
Korea

2013년 7 월29일 남편에게 문자 한통을 받았다.

"여보! 내일 부터 학교 갈 수 있다고 연락이 왔어!" 미국에 온 지 8개월 만에

그리고 대기 명단에 올린지 5개월, 기다리다 지쳐 잊고 있던 소식을 듣게 된 것이다.

긴장과 기대가 동시에 다가오는 순간이었다.

디아나 선생님은 늘 손을 들고 이야기 하길 바라셨다. 하지만 손을 들고 질문을

하거나 대답을 한다는 건 익숙하지 않은 나에게 다소 어려운 동작이었다.

내 개인적 견해로 선생님의 수업을 방해하거나 개개인의 소소한 질문에 대답할 이유가 없다고 생각했기 때문이다.

그러던 어느 날 선생님의 한 마디가 내 생각을 바꾸어 놓는 계기가 되었다.

"틀려도 괜찮아. 그래서 네가 여기 있는 거야. 누군가 잘못을 바로잡아주면 고맙다고 말 하렴. 그렇게 배우는 거야" 별 이야기 아닐지 모르겠지만 난 이

이야기 이후로 답이 틀려도 손을 들고 질문이 있으면 바로바로 물었다. 질문하는 습관은 공부에도 큰 도움이 되었고 더 오래 기억에 남았다. 그리고

한가지 더 선생님은 "아니"라는 말을 잘 쓰지 않으신다. "아니"라는 대답을 하지 않음으로써 내가 틀린 답에 대한 정답을 다시 한번 더 생각하게 해 주신다.

난 어릴 적 그저 그런, 보통의 평범한 학생이었다. 궁금해하거나 문제를 해결하려 하거나 그랬던 적이 별로 없었던 거 같다. 하지만 이곳에선 내 스스로 헤쳐 나가려고 노력하는 인간으로 바뀌게 되었다.

마지막으로 내가 이렇게 글을 쓰므로 선생님께 감사한 마음을 조금이나마 표현하고 싶다. 나는 곧 미국을 떠나게 되지만, 아마 여기서 함께 공부했던 친구들과 선생님은 잊지 못할 것이다.

Pan Fried Pork With Korean Style Onion Sauce

Ingredients :

one pork steak,
1/3 of onion,
2 tbsp of soy sauce,
2 tbsp of apple vinegar,
2 tbsp of water,
1 ½ tbsp of sugar

Pork steak (2 people)

1. Coat pan lightly with cooking spray (Crisco)
2. Fry the pork steak in the pan
3. Fry the cut pieces a little more so that all sides are thoroughly cooked

Onion sauce (2 people)

1. Cut onion into bite size pieces
2. Soak the onions in water 7-10minutes (strong onion's flavor will become less)
3. Prepare another plate
4. Mix two table spoon of soy sauce, apple vinegar, water and one and half spoons of sugar
5. Add onions in the sauce

Jinha Verheyen
South Korea

돼지고기 와 양파소스 (2인 기준)

재료- 돼지고기 목살 또는 스테이크 부위, 양파1/3,간장,식초,물,설탕

돼지고기 (목살, 스테이크 부위)

1. 팬에 기름을 약간 두른 뒤 약한 불에 익힌다.
2. 적당히 익혀지면 한입 크기로 잘라 놓는다.

양파소스

1. 양파를 한입크기로 얇게 썰어 놓는다.
2. 양파를 물에 담가 매운맛이 줄어들게 한다.
3. 다른접시에 간장 두 스푼 + 사과식초 두 스푼 + 물 두 스푼 + 설탕 한 스푼 반을 넣고 섞는다.
4. 양파를 소스에 넣는다.

그리고 준비된 고기와 함께 먹는다.

Jinha Verheyen
South Korea

Suggestions from a former ESL student

My name is Liseth Valbuena and I'm from Venezuela. I'm married to an American soldier and that is the reason why I had to move to the United States of America.

Since I came to this country I knew that I had to learn English because I didn't want to depend on my husband all the time because I didn't know how to speak English.

I decided to start this course, and now after around nine months I can tell you that I completed my ESL course and I feel really satisfied and proud. From the beginning I put all my energy and dedication into it, because learning another language is not easy. You have to have a real desire to learn. If you come to class only to spend some hours here or because your husband wants it, then you will waste your time.

I have to tell you that this course is not easy, not only because you have to study all the lessons, but also because you must come to class almost four hours a day, five days a week for almost nine months. In my case, maybe it seems easier for me to other people because I don't have children. But I had plenty of activities to do, besides the class, that occupied my time. Plus, I don't have my own car and sometimes it was hard too. But I could do it, and you will do it too. Sometimes you have an appointment, or maybe you or your children will feel sick, but those are eventualities. Please don't invent fake excuses not to come to class. Remember that while you are in this course, there are many people outside who want to be in your place in this classroom.

When my teacher asked me if I could write an essay telling you all my experience in this course, of course I said yes. We think that if a student who already finished the complete course from the beginning, tells you what to expect, what to do, what things worked for me, and other things based on my own experience, maybe it will help you to achieve your own goal.

The first thing I want to tell you is not to be scared to ask questions, and don't be scared to make mistakes. Remember that this is not your native **language,** and each time you will have an error the teacher is going to correct you, and you won't see any progress if you are a passive student instead of an active one. Maybe you think that you are learning when you are paying attention to the other students doubts, and that is true, but remember, those are their mistakes not yours, and maybe you will forget the explanation the teacher will give to correct them faster than the explanation to correct your own mistakes.

Another important thing you must do is do your homework every day, even though you think it is not necessary or it is hard, because if the teacher asks you to do something it is because she knows you can do it, and most importantly, she knows you need to do it. But if you really want to improve, do your homework by yourself. Try to review your classes every now and then because if you don't understand one lesson perhaps you will not understand the next one. Try to be always on time in the class, not only because maybe you will miss something important, but also because when you come late you cause distraction and noise and sometimes the other students can't concentrate. Think that this is not a joke or a game; this is a very serious thing to everybody.

In my case I preferred to sit in the front lines of the classroom, because not always but in the majority of the cases people who want to talk more are the people who are seated in the back rows especially the first days. Sometimes people take the back places because they think that maybe the teacher is not aware that they are there . . . don't even think about it. Our teacher is going to learn your names the first day of the class and she will ask questions to everybody, no matter where they are seated. It's preferable if you sit with a partner who doesn't speak your language. That helps you to speak in English if you want to communicate with him or her.

When you have some discussions in class about any topic don't be afraid to say whatever is on your minds, simply try to explain your thoughts in the best way that you can, and trust me . . . little by little you will be better and better each time.

Keep your notes, exercises, homework, etc . . . in a folder. Don't throw away the papers you use here, because you never know when the teacher will ask for something. Take notes in the class even though you don't understand at that moment. You have to study by yourselves at home. Don't limit your

English studies only to this class. The teacher is going to give you the basics but you have to investigate more if you want to improve faster.

In our ESL classes we received visits from some guest speakers who talked about different topics. It was interesting because sometimes you have a problem and you don't know what to do, and those people maybe can help you.

One of the things I enjoyed more was when we watched movies. After that we had discussions about them or sometimes we had to write what the movie was about. It was a big challenge to me because when I started I couldn't write more than one page, and with a lot of mistakes. But at the end I could write many pages, plenty of mistakes too but in a less quantity. It could happen to you too if you will not be afraid to write, and if you will make all your corrections.

In my experience I really enjoyed our field trips, to the Planetarium, to the CTC Campus Tour and to the City Hall in Killeen. Each time I learned different things that maybe many people who have been here in Killeen for many years don't know yet. You have that opportunity, and also it will be free. Don't waste your time, ask questions, be interested and try to listen and understand what the people in those places say to you. Remember, your ears will be accustomed to the way the teacher **speaks**. You have to listen and understand when other people are talking, maybe it will be hard time for many of you, but don't worry about it, you are not the only one. That still happened to me too sometimes.

One of the biggest challenges to me was when we had to create a business project. We had to act and speak in front of an audience, different from our classmates and our teacher. Even though we were afraid, we did it very well.

At the end of the course, please don't expect that you are going to speak as people who have been here for many years, but certainly you are going to be able to maintain a normal conversation at the hospital, in the bank, in the supermarket, and also many of you will be ready to attend college.

Some days maybe you will feel that you are not learning enough, but let me tell you once again trust me, don't feel frustrated, you are going to make it. Suddenly you will speak English and you will not even know when it happened. Of course, you need more than nine months to speak very well but this is the beginning.

I can write ten more pages telling you what to do or what not to do based on my experience, but I think that each person is different. But it will work for everybody if you have the real desire the constant dedication, and the strong determination to do it.

Live your own experience as best as you can. I hope that you will enjoy and you will take advantage of this course as I did.

One last thing, please, please, pleeeaaaseee if some day you can't attend the class please call teacher or at least send her a message, but don't forget to write your name on it.

P.S. Maybe some of you would like to know who the teacher is, but I can't tell you anything, because our teacher doesn't like to hear compliments from us to her. All I have to say about her are good things; she is one of the best **teachers** I have ever had.

Liseth Valbuena
Venezuela

Mi Experiencia Como Estudiante De Ingles Como Segunda Lengua (Esl).

Mi nombre es Liseth Valbuena y soy de Venezuela. Estoy casada con un soldado Americano y esa es la razón por la cual me tuve que mudar a los Estados Unidos de América.

Desde que vine a este país, yo sabía que tenía que aprender Inglés porque no quería depender de mi esposo todo el tiempo por no saber como hablarlo.

Decidí empezar este curso, y ahora despues de alrededor de nueve meses puedo decirles que completé mi curso de ESL y me siento realmente satisfecha y orgullosa de mí. Desde el principio puse todas mis energías y dedicación en esto, porque aprender otro idioma no es fácil. Hay que tener el verdadero deseo de aprender. Si vienen a clase solo para pasar algunas horas aca o porque sus esposos(as) así lo quieren, pues entonces perderán el tiempo.

Tengo que decirles que este curso no es fácil, no solo porque tienen qwue estudiar todas las lecciones, sino porque deben venir a clases de casi cuatro horas al día, cinco veces a la semana, por aproximadamente nueve meses. En mi caso quizás pareciera ser más fácil que para otras personas, porque no tengo hijos. Pero yo tuve muchas otras actividades que hacer además de las clases, que también ocuparon mi tiempo. Además, yo no tengo mi carro propio y muchas veces eso fué difícil también. Algunas veces tendrán una cita, o quizás ustedes o sus hijos se enfermarán, pero esas son eventualidades. Por favor, no inventen falsas excusas para no venir a clases. Recuerden que mientras ustedes están en este curso, hay muchas personas afuera que quisieran estar en sus puestos en este salón de clases.

Cuando mi prosesora me pidió que si podría escribir una carta contándoles a ustedes como fué toda mi experiencia en este curso, por supuesto que dije que si. Nosotras pensamos que sí algún estudiante como yo, que ya terminé el curso complete desde el principio, les dijera que esperar, que hacer, que cosas funcionaron en mí, y otras cosas más basadas en mi propia experiencia, quizás eso les ayudará a ustedes a lograr su objetivo.

La primera cosa que les quiero decir es que no teman hacer preguntas, ni teman cometer errores. Recuerden que éste no es su idioma natal, y además cada vez que cometan un error, la profesora les corregirá, y nunca verán ningún progreso si son un estudiante pasivo en vez de uno activo. Quizás piensen que están aprendiendo cuando prestan atención a las dudas de otros estudiantes, y es cierto, pero recuerden, esas son las dudas de ellos, no las de ustedes, y tal vez olvidarán la explicación que la profesora dará para corregirlos a ellos, más rápido que la explicación que ella dará para corregir sus propios errores.

Otra cosa importante es que deben hacer sus tareas todos los días, a pesar de que piensen que no es necesario o piensen que es difícil, porque sí la profesora les pide hacer algo es porque ella sabe que lo pueden hacer, y más importante es, que ella sabe que ustedes necesitan hacerlo. Pero, sí realmente quieren mejorar, hagan sus tareas ustedes mismos. Traten de repasar sus clases de vez en cuando, porque sí no entienden una lección quizás no entenderán la próxima. Traten de estar siempre puntuales en la clase, no solo porque se pueden perder de algo importante, sino porque cuando llegan tarde causan distracción y ruido y algunas veces los otros estudiantes no pueden estar concentrados debido a eso. Piensen que esto no es una broma, o un juego, esto es algo muy serio para todos.

En mi caso, yo prefer sentarme en las filas de alante del salon de clase, porque no siempre, pero si en la mayoría de los casos, la gente que quiere estar hablando se sienta en las filas de atrás, especialmente los primeros días. Muchas veces la gente se sienta atrás porque piensan que la profesora no está consciente de que están allí . . . ni siquiera piensen en eso. Nuestra profesora se aprenderá todos sus nombres el primer día de clases y hará preguntas a todo el mundo, sin importer donde estén sentados. Es preferable si se sientan con una pareja que no hable su mismo idioma. Eso ayuda a hablar Inglés, sí se quieren comunicar con él o ella.

Cuando hay alguna discussion en clase sobre algún tópico, no teman decir lo que sea que se les venga a la mente, simplemente traten de explicar sus pensamientos de la mejor manera que puedan, y creanme . . . poco a poco estarán mejor y mejor cada vez.

Mantengan sus notas, ejercicios, tareas, etc, en una carpeta. No tiren los papeles que usan acá, porque ustedes nunca sabrán cuando la profesora pedirá algo.

Tomen notas de la clase así no entiendan nada en el momento. Tienen que estudiar por su cuenta en la casa. No limíten sus estudios de Inglés solo a esta clase. La profesora les dará lo básico pero ustedes tienen que investigar más sí quieren progresar más rápido.

En nuestras clases de ESL nosotros recibimos la visita de algunos oradores invitados que nos hablaron de diferentes temas. Fué interesante porque algunas veces tenemos algún problema y no sabemos que hacer, y esas personas quizás pueden ayudarnos.

Una de las cosas que yo disfruté más fué cuando veíamos películas. Después de verlas teníamos discusiones acerca de las mismas y a veces teníamos que escribir de qué trataba la película. Fué un gran reto para mí porque cuando empecé yo no podía escribir más de una hoja, y con muchos errores. Pero al final del curso pude escribir muchas páginas, con muchos errores también, pero menos que antes. Eso les podría pasar a ustedes también sí no tienen miedo de escribir y si hacen todas las correcciones que la profesora les haga.

En mi experiencia, yo realmente disfruté nuestros paseos fuera del salon de clases, al Planetario, a el Tour por el campus de CTC y al Ayuntamiento o Municipio de Killeen. Cada vez aprendí cosas diferentes que quizás mucha gente que ha vivido aca en Killeen por muchos años, no conoce aún. No desperdicien su tiempo alli, hagan preguntas, muestren interés y traten de escuchar y entender lo que la gente en esos sitios les están diciendo. Recuerden que sus oídos estarán acostumbrados a escuchar como habla la profesora. Tienen que escuchar y entender cuando les hablan otras personas, quizás sera difícil para muchos de ustedes, pero no se preocupen, ustedes no son los únicos. Eso me sigue pasando a mí algunas veces.

Uno de los retos más grandes para mí fué cuando tuvimos que crear un proyecto de negocio. Tuvimos que actuar y hablar en frente de una audiencia, diferente a nuestros compañeros de clase y a nuestra profesora. A pesar de que estuvimos asustados, lo hicimos bastante bien.

Al final del curso, por favor no esperen que van a hablar inglés como la gente que ha estado acá por muchos años, pero ciertamente serán capaces de mantener una conversación normal en el hospital, en el banco, en el supermercado y también muchos de ustedes estarán listos para ir a la Universidad.

Algunos días quizás se sentirán que no están aprendiendo suficiente, pero dejenme decirles una vez más, créanme, no se sientan frustrados, lo van a lograr. De repente hablarán inglés y ni siquiera se darán cuenta cuando pasó. Por supuesto, se necesitan más de nueve meses para hablarlo muy bien, pero éste es el comienzo.

Podría escribir diez hojas mas diciéndoles que hacer o que no hacer basado en mi experiencia, pero creo que cada persona es diferente. Pero el curso funcionará en todos sí se tiene el deseo real, la constante dedicación y la fuerte determinación de hacerlo.

Vivan su propia experiencia lo major que puedan. Espero que disfruten y aprovechen éste curso tanto como yo lo híce.

Una última cosa, por favor, por favor, por favooooooooor, sí algún día no pueden venir a clases, por favor llamen a la profesora o al menos envíenle un mensaje, pero no olviden escribir sus nombres en él.

P.D. Quizás muchos de ustedes quisieran saber como es la profesora, pero no puedo decirles nada, porque a nuestra profesora no le gusta escuchar halagos de nosotros hacia ella. Todo lo que tengo que decir acerca de ella son cosas buenas , . . . ella es una de las mejores profesoras que he tenido.

Liseth Valbuena
Venezuela

About the Author

The author, currently an ESL instructor at Central Texas College, Fort Hood, TX. is a candidate for a Master's Degree, International Relations, at St. Mary's University. She was a Journalism Instructor at the Defense Information school, Ft. Meade, MD and Ft. Benjamin Harrison, Indianapolis, Ind. and a Public Affairs Non-Commissioned Officer/Broadcast Journalist with the First Cavalry Division. She is familiar with several languages and graduated in the top ten percent of her Russian language course at the Defense Language Institute, Monterey, CA. She was the editor for the Berlin Observer, Berlin, Germany and various military newspapers in the United States. She has written poems, in brochure format, and articles for military newspapers in Germany and the United States.